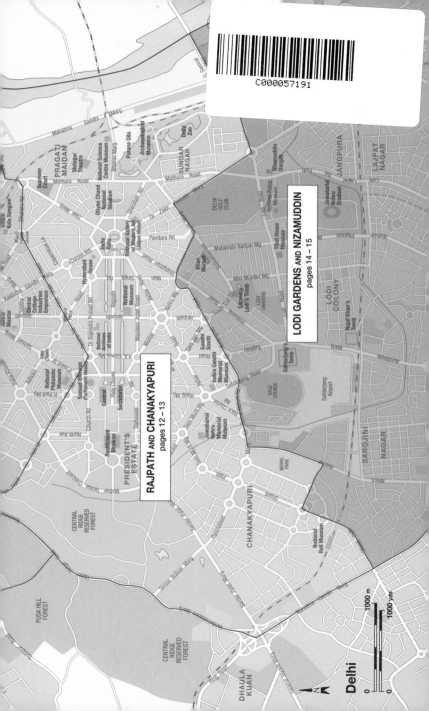

RAJPATH AND CHANAKYAPURI
pages 12 – 13

LODI GARDENS AND NIZAMUDDIN
pages 14 – 15

Delhi

C000057191

INSIGHT GUIDES

DELHI
smart guide

APA PUBLICATIONS L

Part of the Langenscheidt Publishing Group

Contents

Areas

A–Z

Below: roses on their way to market.

Contents

Below: pashmina shawls for sale in a government emporium.

Delhi

Delhi is the political and administrative centre of the world's largest democracy. Strategically located between the Aravalli hills and the Yamuna river, its site has been occupied for millennia. It has survived invasion, sacking and a political 'emergency' to emerge as a fascinating mix of ancient and modern, and has a new-found sense of pride and energy.

Delhi Facts and Figures

Population: **18 million**
Population including the adjoining cities in Haryana and Uttar Pradesh: **25 million**
Area: **1,483 sq km (573 sq miles)**
Highest point: **Bhatti, 318 m (1,043 ft)**
Number of villages: **165**
Population density: **12,137 people per sq km (31,413 per sq mile)**
Gender ratio: **821 females to 1,000 males**
Literacy: **82 percent**
Population living below the poverty line: **9 percent**
Number of cars: **1.6 million**
Number of auto rickshaws: **over 70,000**

Origins and Growth

The first city on the site of modern Delhi was Indraprastha, the legendary Pandava capital of the *Mahabharata*. Excavations at the Purana Qila date this to arount the st century BC. Next came Lal Kot, founded in the 8th century AD by Tomara and then Chauhan Rajputs. The Muslim Delhi Sultanate built the Qutb Minar complex, Siri and then Tughlaqabad, all in the south. The next city, Firozabad, was followed by those of the Sayyids and the Lodis, whose tombs stand in Lodi Gardens. The Mughals took over, and their legacy is Shahjahanabad, also known as 'Old' Delhi. They were supplanted by the British, and between 1911–31 'New' Delhi was designed by Edwin Lutyens and Herbert Baker.

This sprawling city has two centres, Old and New Delhi, and a series of ancient villages and sites that have been engulfed by newer residential areas (known as colonies). These newer areas mostly lie either to the south (where Delhi extends for many kilometres) and across the border into the neighbouring state of Haryana, where the city of Gurgaon forms a de-facto Delhi suburb, or on the eastern side of the Yamuna such as NOIDA (the New Okhla Industrial Development Authority, established by Sanjay Gandhi).

Problems and Progress

During the 1990s and early years of this century the city struggled to cope with the effects of its rapid expansion – pollution, traffic congestion, shortages of water and power, continual construction – and an extreme climate. However, more recently Delhi has reinvented itself as one of the most forward- thinking and best-run cities in India. Pollution was greatly curbed by the 2001 order of the Supreme Court that forced all public transport to convert from running on diesel to compressed natural gas (CNG), although air quality has now returned to pre-CNG levels due to the massive increase in private vehicle ownership, most of which is non-CNG. Delhi's popular Chief Minister Shiela Dixit must also take much of the credit: her administration has clamped down on illegal building, attempted to clean up the city's streets and pushed major infrastructure projects. The most prominent of these is the new

Below: flowers decorate a rickshaw.

metro system. The construction of the metro, supervised by the highly efficient E. Sreedharan, has garnered countrywide praise for its swift progress and lack of corruption.

A further boost to the city came when it was awarded the 2010 Commonwealth Games. Although the games have been used as an excuse for much-needed infrastructure works – including a new international airport close to the existing Indira Gandhi Airport – some of this development has been carried at the expense of the poor. Large areas of slums have been cleared and people dispossesed of what little they had, in the name of beautifying the city.

Delhi is now the most expensive place to live in India and has overtaken Mumbai as the most desirable place to move to in the country, attracting a greater influx of people than its great rival. While Mumbai remains the undisputed centre of finance, Delhi is not only the political centre but increasingly the centre of much of India's cultural life, home to many of the country's top fashion designers, as well as its writers, artists and musicians. It is also has a booming retail sector, with glossy new malls springing up all the time and numerous chic little boutiques in its colony markets. India's largest mall, no doubt soon to be surpassed by an even larger construction, lies just over the state boundary in Gurgaon, where many of the newly thriving middle classes have their homes.

Highlights

▲ **Rajpath** The crowning glory of the British city is Lutyens's and Baker's centre of government.

▶ **Lal Qila** Delhi's Mughal fort is replete with shady pavilions and impressive ramparts.

▲ **Humayun's Tomb** This Mughal tomb, a Unesco World Heritage Site, was the model for the Taj Mahal in Agra.

▶ **Lodi Gardens** This beautifully maintained stretch of greenery in the city centre contains a number of important monuments.

▲ **Qutb Minar Complex** The earliest Islamic monuments in India are truly impressive.

▶ **Jama Masjid** Delhi's main mosque is a masterpiece.

Connaught Place

In many ways, the circular roads of Connaught Place form the hub of Delhi. Just to the north lies the old Mughal capital of Shahjahanabad, while to the south is the centre of government, and beyond are the colonies of the ever-expanding city, now all linked by the new metro with its interchange at Rajiv Chowk. For most people it remains the logical place to start their exploration of the city and although, with a couple of exceptions, the area does not contain Delhi's most interesting cultural or historical sights, there are a number of important religious buildings, and it is a good place to begin a shopping trip.

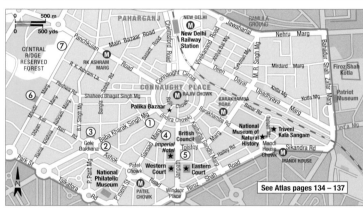

See Atlas pages 134 – 137

Left: shopping in CP.

The Commercial Centre

Although everyone still refers to the concentric rings of shops and offices at the centre of Lutyens's Delhi by its old name of **Connaught Place** (or 'CP' for short), the main outer and inner roads have been renamed Indira Chowk and Rajiv Chowk respectively. Designed by the architect Robert Tor Russell as the commerical hub of the New City, and at one time home to exclusive shops and elegant cafés, Connaught Place is now an odd mixture of run-down seediness and contemporary chic. There are popular new bars, restaurants and chain stores, as well as a metro station, but the area suffers from a lack of protection from development which many say has destroyed the gentility of the once peaceful arcades.

The Delhi authorities have been trying to restore a number of the buildings. However, their efforts are being botched by poor work and what appears to be behind-the-scenes pressure from developers who are keen to get their hands on this area of prime real estate.

Left: the Lakshmi
Narayan Mandir.

Delhi's most important cultural
institutions, inlcuding the
Triveni Kala Sangam with its
gallery and theatre and the
national institutes of music,
literature and the fine arts.
SEE ALSO HOTELS, P.60; LITERATURE
AND THEATRE, P.73; MONUMENTS,
P.74; MUSEUMS AND GALLERIES,
P.84; RELIGIONS AND RELIGIOUS
SITES, P.106; SHOPPING, P.122

New Delhi Station

Directly to the north of
Connaught Place is **New
Delhi Station** (the city has
several railway stations), one
of the busiest and most important in all of India, handling
over 350,000 passengers
every day. It was renovated in
time for the 2010 Common-
wealth Games, and while the
interior is much improved, the
outside is as chaotic as ever.

Close by is the notorious
backpacker's haunt of **Pahar-
ganj**. This unattractive district
of fleapit hotels, touts and
suspect eating places is one
of the latest districts to come
under the scrutiny of the city
authorities, and, in an effort to
clean it up, a number of the
more disreputable places
have been closed down.

The Lakshmi Temple

The area to the west of
Connaught Place is a little
quieter. The main sight here is
the **Lakshmi Narayan Mandir**
⑥, one of the most popular
temples in Delhi. To the north
of the temple, also on Mandir
Marg, is the red-brick, Modernist **St Thomas's Church**
⑦. Behind both of these
religious buildings is part
of the **Central Ridge
Reserved Forest**.
SEE ALSO PARKS AND GARDENS,
P.100; RELIGIONS AND
RELIGIOUS SITES, P.106

Bungalows and Boulevards

To the south of Connaught
Place the wide boulevards of
Lutyens's planned city run
down to the centre of government around Rajpath. As well
as government offices, here
are some of Lutyens's and
Baker's famed Delhi
bungalows. There are five
main roads, beginning in the
west with **Baba Kharak
Singh Marg**. This is the location of many of the government-run emporia that sell
handicrafts from each of
India's states. Opposite these
is the Hindu **Hanuman
Mandir** ①, while further
down, on the corner of Ashok
Road, is the ornate and popular **Bangla Sahib Gurudwara** ②. Also here is the
Sacred Heart Cathedral ③,
Delhi's most important
Catholic church.

To the east, **Sansad Marg**
is the location of the strange-
looking **Jantar Mantar** ④, Jai

Singh's astronomical observatory. The long, straight reach
of Janpath is where you will
find the **Central Cottage
Industries Emporium** ⑤,
cousin of the emporia on
Baba Kharak Singh Marg but
by far the largest – effectively
a department store of handicrafts from all over India.
Opposite this is the elegant
Imperial Hotel – the only
hotel to be included in
Lutyens's plans for the city.
Beside the hotel is the **Western Court** building and across
the road the **Eastern Court**,
designed, like Conaught
Place, by R.T. Russell.

East of **Kasturba Gandhi
Marg**, location of the British
Council Building designed by
Charles Correa and the Max
Müller Bhavan, is
Barakhamba Road. This leads
down to the roundabout of
Mandi House Chowk. As
well as being the site of the
**National Museum of Natural
History**, here are a number of

Old Delhi and Raj Ghat

Once a beautifully laid-out Mughal city, with gardens hidden behind the high walls of opulent *havelis* and water flowing through the centre of its bazaars, Old Delhi – or Shahjahanabad, after its founder – is still a fascinating place to explore, even if its former glory is sometimes hard to imagine. As well as containing the Lal Qila and Jama Masjid, two of the most important monuments of Mughal India, its streets and markets teem with life and occasionally reveal a glimpse of the refined Muslim culture for which it was once famous. Close by are the cremation grounds of the leaders of Independent India, and the ruins of one of Delhi's first cities.

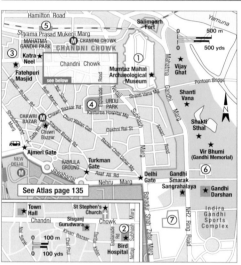

Mahal fame – as the capital of the Mughal empire in 1638. In this year the outer defences of the city's fort and imperial palace were built. The site, known as the **Lal Qila** ① (or Red Fort) is still one of the most impressive pieces of architecture in Delhi.
SEE ALSO FORTS, P.54

Chandni Chowk and the Bazaars

Opposite the Lahore Gate, the main entrance to the Lal Qila, is **Chandni Chowk** (named after the 'Moonlight Square', in front of the 19th-century Town Hall, that once had a beautiful pool), a long, wide and now very busy street. It is hard to imagine now, but when it was first laid out the Nahr-i-Bihisht, or 'Stream of Paradise', that flowed from the palace used to make its way down the centre of the road.

There is a surprising mixture of places of worship along the street. The **Jain Mandir** ② famously contains a bird hospital, and there is also the **Sisganj Gurudwara** and **St Stephen's Church** here. At the far end of the streeet, past the **Town Hall** built in 1864, is the 17th-century **Fatehpuri Masjid**. Beyond the mosque is **Khari Baoli** ③, the largest spice market in Asia.

The Lal Qila (Red Fort)

The Mughal city of Delhi, properly known as Shahjahanabad and more commonly as Old Delhi, is a crowded and busy area of narrow streets and bazaars. Within the boundaries of the old city walls, mostly no longer standing, there are some of the most important Mughal monuments in the city. Shahjahanabad was founded by the ruler Shah Jahan – of Taj

Left: a decorated doorway.

Left: in the fabric bazaar of Katra Neel.

The northern edge of Shahjahanabad runs above the neo-Gothic **Delhi Railway Station** ⑤ (also known as Old Delhi Station) built by the British in 1867.
SEE ALSO FORTS, P.55; MONUMENTS, P.74, 75, 76

Raj Ghat and Firoz Shah Kotla

To the east of Old Delhi, between the Lal Qila and the banks of the Yamuna, is **Raj Ghat** ⑥. This area of landscaped parkland is where the deceased leaders of Independent India have been cremated. They are now commemorated by a series of memorials. The largest of these remembers Gandhi, to whom there is also a museum, the **Gandhi Darshan**, on the site.

To the southwest of Raj Ghat is part of Firozabad, one of the settlements of the 14th-century Tughlaq dynasty. **Firoz Shah Kotla** ⑦ is a large ruined fort. Within its walls is an Ashokan pillar.
SEE ALSO FORTS, P.54; MONUMENTS, P.75; MUSEUMS AND GALLERIES, P.85; PARKS AND GARDENS, P.98

Traditionally, different streets were reserved for different occupations, and this can still be seen in the bazaars that fan out from Chandni Chowk. Opposite the famous sweet-sellers **Ghantewala**, the narrow lane of **Kinari Bazaar** (selling tinsel and braid) leads into **Dariba Kalan**, the street of the jewellers. Beyond the Town Hall is the maze of stalls and shops of **Katra Neel**, the fabric bazaar, while opposite is the street of **Nai Sarak**, given over to printers and booksellers. At the end of Nai Sarak is **Chawri Bazaar**, off which is the amazing spare-car-parts bazaar.
SEE ALSO FOOD AND DRINK, P.52, 53; RELIGIONS AND RELIGIOUS SITES, P.107, 108; SHOPPING, P.120

The Jama Masjid

Chawri Bazaar leads up to the **Jama Masjid** ④, the largest mosque in India. This was commissioned by Shah Jahan and sits on a small hill to the south of the Lal Qila, giving it a commanding position over its surroundings.
SEE ALSO RELIGIONS AND RELIGIOUS SITES, P.107

The City Gates

The walls of Shahjahanabad originally had 14 main gateways, of which five still survive. To the south, on the edge of New Delhi, are the **Delhi** and **Ajmeri Gates**. Just outside the latter is the late-17th-century *madarsa* and tomb of Ghaziuddin, a minister at the court of Aurangzeb.

Between the Delhi and Ajmeri Gates is the **Turkman Gate**. The two remaining gates lie to the north above **Salimgarh Fort** on the edge of the British Civil Lines *(see pages 10–11)*.

Right: the Gandhi memorial at Raj Ghat.

North Delhi

The British legacy to the city is not only that of the New Delhi of Lutyens and Baker. The first district established by the British was to the north of the Mughal city of Shahjahanabad, where you can still find their grand administrative buildings, the earliest church still standing in Delhi, as well as many reminders of the fierce fighting that took place here during the Uprising of 1857. This is particularly commemorated on the forested Northern Ridge that bisects this part of the city. On the far side of the Ridge are some of Delhi's most revered educational institutions and a beautiful Mughal garden.

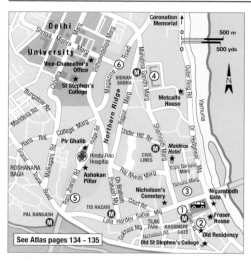

See Atlas pages 134 – 135

Around Kashmere Gate

To the north of Shahjahanabad is the site of the first British settlement in Delhi. Known as the **Civil Lines**, it is tucked between the forest and scrub of the Northern Ridge and the Yamuna river. The main gateway between the Civil Lines and Old Delhi is **Kashmere Gate** ①.

South of Kashmere Gate on Lothian Road is **St James's Church** ②, the oldest church in Delhi. The church was commissioned by James Skinner, and his grave is just in front of the altar. Also on Lothian Road is the **Old Residency**. Taken over by the British in 1803, it was once part of the palace of Dara Shikoh, the eldest son of Shah Jahan.

Two other buildings of interest are in the area: the first is the **House of William Fraser**, Resident of Delhi in 1833, with its large dome (now used by the Indian Railways); the second is the original building of **St Stephen's College**. This was designed by Samuel Swinton Jacob in 1891 and is currently used by the Election Commission.

To the east, beside the river, is another of the remaining gateways in the old city walls, the **Nigambodh Gate**, close to the cremation *ghat* from which it takes it name.

A rather more prosaic site can be found next to Kashmere Gate, the **Inter State Bus Terminal** (ISBT). Rather old, it is a large, confusing and run-down place. In an attempt to take some of the pressure off this central site, a number of services have been transferred to the terminals in Sarai Kale Khan and Anand Vihar.

To the north of Kashmere Gate, on the other side of the road from the ISBT, is **Qudsia Bagh** ③, a garden laid out by Qudsia Begum during the 18th century, part of which has now been taken over by the Masons. The other patches of greenery in the area are **Tilak Park** on Lala Hardev Sahai Marg and, opposite, **Nicholson's Cemetery**.

SEE ALSO MONUMENTS, P.77; PARKS AND GARDENS, P.98, 99; RELIGIONS AND RELIGIOUS SITES, P.108

The Civil Lines

Before the building of New Delhi the area to the north was the location of a number

Left: Kashmere Gate.

ings, including the Vice-Chancellor's Office, in its well-maintained grounds. Close by is **St Stephen's College**, Delhi's poshest school. It moved here from its earlier site when the university opened in 1922.

Southwest of St Stephen's, just off the Grand Trunk Road, is the **Roshanara Bagh**, a garden laid out by Shah Jahan's youngest daughter.
SEE ALSO MONUMENTS, P.76, 77; PARKS AND GARDENS, P.99

Further Afield

To the north of the Ridge, out beyond the **Majnu ka Tila Gurudwara**, and beside the Outer Ring Road, is the site of the British durbars of 1877, 1903 and 1911, now used as a dumping ground for British monumental statuary thought inappropriate for the capital of an independent India. The area is known as **Coronation Memorial** and takes its name from the large statue of George V that originally stood at India Gate. Even further out, beyond the city at **Shalimar Bagh**, is another Mughal garden, this one laid out by the emperor Shah Jahan in 1653.
SEE ALSO MONUMENTS, P.76; PARKS AND GARDENS, P.99

of British institutions. Here is the neoclassical **Maiden's Hotel**, built in 1900, and the **Old Secretariat building** ④. Built in 1912, this was a temporary home for the British adminstration before New Delhi was completed; it now houses the Delhi Assembly. To the east of these is the **Metcalfe House**, built in the early 19th century by Sir Thomas Metcalfe, a commissioner of the city.
SEE ALSO HOTELS, P.62

The Northern Ridge

Overlooking the Civil Lines is the Northern Ridge. At its southern end is the neo-Gothic **Mutiny Memorial** ⑤ commemorating the soldiers killed in 1857.

A little way to the north, along Rani Jhansi Road, is a rather worn **Ashokan Pillar**, placed here in 1867. By the pillar is the **Hindu Rao Hospital**. This mansion was originally built by William

Fraser, but after he was murdered in 1835 it became a hospital. In its grounds is the **Pir Ghalib**, a ruined hunting lodge built by Firoz Shah Tughlak.

At the far end of the Ridge is the **Flagstaff Tower** ⑥, marking the spot where the British women and children retreated to during the 1857 Uprising.

On the western side of the Ridge is the main campus of **Delhi University** with a number of notable British build-

The Royal Durbar of 1911 was held to commemorate the coronation of George V, so it is apt that the statue of the king is now on the site *(right)*. It was attended by 562 maharajas from the so-called Princely States (each maharaja was accompanied by an average of 5.8 wives). It was at the durbar that the king announced the moving of the capital to Delhi.

Rajpath and Chanakyapuri

One of the aims of Lutyens was to build a fitting capital for the jewel in the crown of the 'empire on which the sun will never set'. Well, this prediction did not come true, but his city of New Delhi remains one of the world's greatest examples of urban planning, and has provided a suitably grand setting for the government of an independent India. As well as the wide avenues on which impressive buildings house the president, parliament and important ministries – all sights in their own right – this area contains some of the city's best museums, parks and statues, and the first Mughal fort in Delhi.

The Centre of Power

If Connaught Place is the commercial hub of Delhi then **Rajpath** is not only the political hub of the city but also the whole country. This centrepiece of Lutyens's grand design was an impressive conception, intended to show off the full pomp and might of the British empire. Rajpath is a long, straight boulevard, laid out on the plain to the south of Shahjahabad, rising to the small hill of Raisina at its western end. Along its length are India's most important government buildings, as well as the national collections of art and archaeology.

India Gate

At the far eastern end of Rajpath is the imposing monumental arch of **India Gate** ①, a memorial to the dead of the Indian Army. Behind India Gate is the **Dayan Chand National Stadium**, venue for the men's hockey world cup in 2010.

The hexagonal pattern of streets that surrounds India Gate was designated as the Princes' Area. Large mansions were constructed for each of the most important rulers of the Princely States.

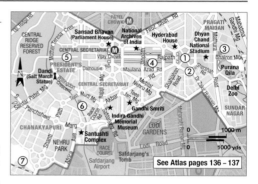

See Atlas pages 136 – 137

Rashtrapati Bhavan was set on top of Raisina Hill so that its vast dome might dominate the whole view along Rajpath. However, Herbert Baker *(see p26)* wanted North and South Blocks to inhabit the high ground as well, and so Rashtrapati Bhavan was pushed back 1,200 m (3,937 ft). The unforeseen consequence of this was that as you approach the hill Rashtrapati Bhavan gradually disappears from view. This was noticed too late, and the mistake was something for which Lutyens never forgave the younger architect.

Among these were the rulers of Hyderabad, Bikaner, Baroda and Jaipur. Their Delhi residences were taken over by the government at Independence, and the most impressive, **Hyderabad House** (designed by Lutyens), is used for banquets and housing visiting dignitaries. Jaipur House now contains the **National Gallery of Modern Art** ②.

SEE ALSO MONUMENTS, P.78; MUSEUMS AND GALLERIES, P.88; SPORT, P.125

Pragati Maidan and the Purana Qila

To the east of the India Gate hexagon, towards the Yamuna, is **Pragati Maidan**, Delhi's exhibition ground. Of more interest to visitors, however, is the excellent **Crafts Museum** ③ tucked away in its southwestern corner.

Opposite the Crafts Museum is the **Purana Qila**

Left: the gates to Rashtrapati Bhavan.

address is **7 Race Course Road**, home of the prime minister.

Three museums near here pay tribute to India's past leaders: the **Jawaharlal Nehru Memorial Museum** ⑥ at Teen Murti Bhavan, his daughter Indira Gandhi on **Safdarjang Road**, and the **Gandhi Smriti** at the Birla House on Tees January Marg. SEE ALSO MUSEUMS AND GALLERIES, P.87, 88; POLITICS, P.102

Chanakyapuri

To the southwest of Rashtrapti Bhavan is the very pleasant diplomatic enclave of **Chanakyapuri**, home to the majority of foreign embassies and diplomatic missions in the capital. To the west is the **Central Ridge** with its parks and reserved forest. On the corner of Sardar Patel Marg and Willingdon Crescent is the **Dandi March Statue** commemorating the famous salt march of Gandhi.

As well being home to the **National Rail Museum** ⑦, Chanakyapuri also has the **Santushti** shopping complex and the nearby **Nehru Park**. SEE ALSO MONUMENTS, P.77; MUSEUMS AND GALLERIES, P.89; PARKS AND GARDENS, P.100; SHOPPING, P.121

(Old Fort). Although there had been settlement on the site for centuries, its present form was first laid down by the emperor Humayun in 1538.

Beyond the Purana Qila is **Delhi Zoo** and the upmarket residential and shopping colony of **Sundar Nagar**. SEE ALSO CHILDREN, P.35; FORTS, P.56; MUSEUMS AND GALLERIES, P.87

Rajpath and Raisina Hill

Heading west down Rajpath from India Gate, the wide, park-lined road is flanked by more institutions of state, such as the **National Archives**. Where Janpath crosses Rajpath, on the southern side of the junction, a large building houses the **National Museum** ④, India's premier collection of archaeological and historical artefacts.

Further along, on the right-hand side and just off Rajpath near the Central Secretariat metro station, is the circular **Sansad Bhavan**,

India's parliament building. From here on Rajpath turns into Vijay Chowk and rises up between the Secretariat buildings, known by everyone as **North and South Blocks**, housing the Home Affairs and Finance Ministries and the External Affairs Ministry respectively.

Beyond the Secretariat is the great domed **Rashtrapati Bhavan** ⑤, built as the Viceroy's house but now home to the President of India. SEE ALSO MUSEUMS AND GALLERIES, P.88

Museums and Memorials

To the south of Rajpath is the heartland of the distinctive bungalows designed by Lutyens and Baker, many of which are home to senior politicians, bureaucrats and members of India's armed forces. The most famous

Right: an exhibit at the National Rail Museum.

13

Lodi Gardens and Nizamuddin

The inner 'colonies' that cover the area between New Delhi and the southern portion of the Ring Road are some of the most attractive and interesting parts of the city. As well as beautiful parks and local market areas (the location of some of Delhi's best designer boutiques and some excellent restaurants), the area is dotted with impressive monuments, including a Unesco World Heritage Site, as well as containing one of the most important Muslim shrines in India.

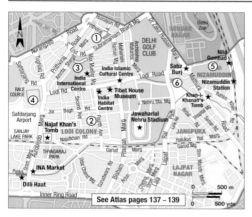

Above: books at Khan Market.

Colonies and Markets

The discrete areas to the south of New Delhi are known as 'colonies', referring either to villages that were swallowed up as the city expanded or to planned residential communities. Highly sought after as places to live, they contain notable cultural and academic institutions as well as some of the best shopping areas in Delhi.

Of these areas, known as markets, though they do not resemble them in the traditional sense, two of the best are **Khan Market** ① on Subramaniam Bharti Road and **Lodi Colony Market** ② just off Lodi Road. To the south,

just before Aurobindo Marg hits the Ring Road, is **Dilli Haat**, a government-run crafts market, and across the road **INA Market**, the large complex of Delhi's main fruit, veg and meat market.
SEE ALSO SHOPPING, P. 123

Lodi Gardens

Between Khan Market and Lodi Colony are the lovely **Lodi Gardens** ③. One of the city's 'lungs', this well-maintained park was laid out in the 1930s around the **tombs** of the Lodi and Sayyid sultans who ruled over Delhi in the 15th and 16th centuries. The park is also the location of one of the city's most attrac-

tive restaurants: **Lodi – The Garden Restaurant**.

Lodi Road runs along the southern edge of the gardens. Facing them is the **India Habitat Centre**, a beautifully designed cultural and conference centre. Just along from the centre, in the Institutional Area, is the **Tibet House Museum**.

There are two other cultural institutes in the area. On Lodi road is the tiled façade of the **India Islamic Cultural Centre**. Nearby is the **India International Centre**, haunt of Delhi's intellectuals and academics and which it is notoriously hard to join.
SEE ALSO MONUMENTS, P.79; MUSEUMS AND GALLERIES, P.90; PARKS AND GARDENS, P.100; RESTAURANTS, P.117

Safdarjang

At the far western end of Lodi Road, on the other side of

Left: Bara Gumbad in Lodi Gardens.

complex. The most important Muslim pilgrimage site in Delhi, the narrow streets of the area have always thronged with devotees.

Other monuments within the area include **Atgah Khan's Tomb** and the marble **Chaunsath Khamba**. Next door to the latter is the **Ghalib Academy**, the library and tomb of the great 19th-century Urdu poet. A little way to the south is the early Mughal tomb of **Khan-i-Khanan**, a member of the court of Akhbar.

SEE ALSO MONUMENTS, P.78, 79; MUSEUMS AND GALLERIES, P.89; RELIGIOUS SITES, P.109

Sports Grounds

As well as being awash with Mughal remains, this part of Delhi has a number of the city's most prestigious sports facilities. Foremost among them is **Delhi Golf Club**, a rather chi-chi establishment for Delhi's elite, but with beautiful grounds. To the south is **Jawaharlal Nehru Stadium**, which underwent a major make-over for the 2010 Commonwealth Games, during which it hosted the opening and closing ceremonies, as well as the athletics. Finally, behind Safdarjang Airport, is **Delhi Race Course**.

SEE ALSO SPORT, P.124, 125

Safdarjang Airport was where Sanjay Gandhi, son of prime minister Indira Gandhi, took off in June 1980. While trying to perform a loop-the-loop in his light aircraft the plane plummeted to the ground and he was killed. Sanjay was deeply unpopular due to his role in the Emergency *(see Politics, p.102–3)* and rumours soon spread that his plane had been tampered with to bump him off.

Aurobindo Marg is **Safdarjang's Tomb** ④, one of the last Mughal garden tombs to be built in Delhi. Further south along Aurobindo Marg is another, slightly later, tomb, this one of **Najaf Khan**, a Persian noble who served at the court of Muhammad Shah.

Opposite Najaf Khan's tomb is **Safdarjang Airport**, once the main Delhi airport but now only used by private light aircraft.

SEE ALSO MONUMENTS, P.80

Humayun's Tomb

At the eastern end of Lodi Road is Delhi's most important Mughal monument, **Humayun's Tomb** ⑤. A Unesco World Heritage Site, it is said to be the prototype for the Taj Mahal in Agra.

Set in the middle of the roundabout just before the tomb is the blue-tiled **Sabz Burj** tomb. Just outside the complex, by the railway, is another tiled tomb, the **Nila Gumbad**. Just down from here is **Nizamuddin Station**, the third of Delhi's main railway stations.

SEE ALSO MONUMENTS, P.78, 80

Nizammuddin

The area's name Nizamuddin comes from that of a Chisti saint, the Sufi Sheikh Nizamuddin Auliya, whose *dargah* ⑥, or tomb, lies just to the west of the Humayun's Tomb

Right: women devotees outside Nizamuddin's tomb.

15

South Delhi

Beyond the Inner Ring Road lies the huge swathe of South Delhi. Even more than the area around Lodi Gardens it consists of separate villages – some still slighty 'rural' in feel – and newer residential colonies, incuding some of the richest areas of Delhi, with upmarket shopping and good bars and restaurants. Although the sights are more spread out than those to the north, highlights include a tomb and *madrasa* of the Delhi sultanates in Hauz Khas Village, and a spectacular lotus-shaped temple. To the west lie Delhi's airports, including the large new terminal and runway being built for the 2010 Commonwealth Games.

See Atlas pages 138 – 139

Hauz Khas Village

Aurobindo Marg continues south from Dilli Haat, running under the Inner Ring Road by the well-maintained roadside gardens planted in memory of Rajiv Gandhi. Immediately on the left heading south is the **All India Institute of Medical Sciences**, one of the country's top hospitals and medical research establishments, and opposite the equally large **Safdarjang Hospital**.

About 1.5 km (1 mile) further on, on the right is the turn-off to **Hauz Khas Village** ①. Set in a large area of parkland, much of which is a **Deer Park**, this small settlement takes its name from the tank (artifical lake for drinking water and irrigation) dug under the rule of Alauddin Khilji in 1300 to supply Siri Fort to the east.

As well as the attractive narrow streets and the shops

Above: an interactive exhibit at the Museum of Toilets.

and galleries, there are some notable early monuments here. The *madrasa* and **tomb** of Firoz Shah Tughlaq lie on the banks of the *hauz khas* ('royal tank').

SEE ALSO MONUMENTS, P.80; PARKS AND GARDENS, P.101

To the far west, out beyond the airport in Mahavir Enclave, is one of Delhi's more unusual museums, the **Sulabh International Museum of Toilets** *(see also Museums and Galleries, p.90)*. The admirable Sulabh Sanitation Movement that runs the museum was set up by Dr Bindeshwar Pathak. It campaigns to improve the dire condition of sanitation in India and end the practice of scavenging (low-caste workers clearing away human waste).

Siri Fort and the Asian Games Village

To the east, just off Khel Gaon Marg, is **Siri Fort** ②. Very little remains of the large 14th-century settlement, but also here is the **Asian Games Village** complex, built for the 1982 games and

Left: stopping for a chat in a South Delhi shopping mall.

Kailash and Kailash Hills. Here you will find the extraordinary **Baha'i Lotus Temple** ⑥. Set in well-maintained gardens, this marble-clad structure is the headquarters of the followers of the Iranian religious teacher Bahá'u'lláh, usually known as the Bahá'is.

Close by is another place of worship, this time the Hindu **Kalkaji Mandir** ⑦, sacred to the goddess Kalka Devi. This popular temple dates back to the 18th century, but much of the present structure is more recent. Even so, it is an interesting place to visit and to see the worshippers at the devotions.

Beyond East of Kailash, on the far side of the railway tracks and bordering Mathura Road, are **Friends Colony** and **Maharani Bagh**, more middle-class residential complexes. New Friends Colony has a number of popular bars and clubs that are worth a visit if you are in the area.

SEE ALSO RELIGIONS AND RELIGIOUS SITES, P.109, 110

Below: the marble-clad 'sails' of the Baha'i Lotus Temple.

extensively renovated for the 2010 Commonwealth Games. Designed by Raj Rewal, the well-conceived housing project takes its cue from the tightly packed cube-like construction of traditional Indian urban architecture.

Between Aurobindo and Khel Gaon Margs are some rather more substantial defensive remains. The **Chor Minar** (literally 'thieves' tower') was built by the Khiljis, and it is thought it was used to display the severed heads of miscreants who had been executed.

To the north of Siri Fort, also just off Khel Gaon Marg, is one of the first air-conditioned malls in Delhi, **Ansal Plaza** ③. Much loved by the middle class who come here to eat and shop in the Western chain stores, it seems to have maintained its place alongside the super-malls that have sprung up further south.

Not far from Ansal Plaza, behind Uday Park, is the **Moth ki Masjid** ④. This delicately built mosque dates from the Lodi period.

SEE ALSO FORTS, P.56; MONUMENTS, P.80; RELIGIOUS SITES, P.110

Greater Kailash I and Nehru Place

The two upmarket residential colonies of **Greater Kailash I** (also known as GK I) and **Nehru Place** lie to the east of Siri Fort. While there are no sights as such to explore, the **M and N Block Markets** ⑤ in Greater Kailash I make a worthwhile shopping excursion and the colonies are also the location of some decent restaurants and bars.

The Lotus Temple and Kalkaji Mandir

To find the area's top 'sights' you have to head a little further east into East of

Mehrauli and Tughlaqabad

The Outer Ring Road divides the exclusive colonies of South Delhi, one of the most expensive places to live in the whole country, from the monument-laden areas around the Unesco World Heritage Site of the Qutb Minar and the fort at Tughlaqabad. These impressive remains bear testimony to the power and wealth of the Delhi Sultanates and more than repay the trip out from the city centre. Sandwiched between these two are the upmarket overspill residential areas of Greater Kailash II and Chitaranjan Park with their good restaurants and bars. To the south there are further gardens and museums to explore.

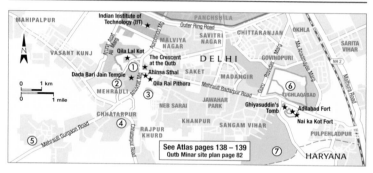

The Qutb Minar Complex

The Outer Ring Road runs directly below the southern boundary of the Hauz Khas deer park. On the far side of the road is the prestigious Delhi branch of the **Indian Institute of Technology** (IIT), the country's premier scientific teaching and research institute. Graduate places here are highly sought after, and a qualification from IIT practically guarantees a well-paid job.

To the south of IIT, at the point where Aurobindo Marg turns into the Mehrauli-Gurgaon Road, is the turn-off to the **Qutb Minar** ①. At the junction, overlooking the archaeological park, is the posh shopping centre **The**

Crescent at the Qutb, a good place to search out some of Delhi's top designers.

Dominating the nearby World Heritage Site, the Qutb itself is a huge minaret built to commemorate the victory of Muhammad of Ghori over the Tomars in 1192. Numerous other important monuments can be found on the

site, including the **Quwwat-ul-Islam** mosque, the mysterious **iron pillar** and the tomb of **Iltutmish**, one of the earliest rulers of the Delhi Sultanate.

SEE ALSO ARCHITECTURE, P.24; MONUMENTS, P.82

Mehrauli Village

Bordering the southern edge of the Qutb Minar Complex is the village of Mehrauli. The ruins of **Lal Kot** ②, Delhi's first city, are spread out across the area. Among the most important monuments here is the octagonal tomb of Adham Khan known as the **Bhulbhulaiyan**. As well as the lovely *baoli* (step well), also worth searching out are the dargah of **Qutbuddin Bakhtiyar Kaki** and the nearby marble **Moti Masjid**.

Right: delicate carving at the Qutb Minar.

18

Left: the impressive ramparts of Tughlaqabad fort.

South of Tughlaqabad and just over the border into neighbouring Harayana, the tank at **Suraj-kund** marks the position of the 11th-century Tomar capital of Surajpal, as well as what was thought to be an early temple to the sun god Surya. A peaceful site, it is a pleasant retreat for anyone in need of an escape from the city. A crafts fair is held here every February.

Tughlaqabad

Far over to the south east of Delhi, just to the north of the Mehrauli-Badarpur Road, are the extensive 14th-century ruins of **Tughlaqabad Fort** ⑥. The tomb of the builder of the fort, **Ghiyasuddin**, lies just to the south of the walls, while close by are the ruins of the much smaller forts of **Nai ka Kot** and **Adilabad**.

The open area that spans the Delhi-Haryana border between Tughlaqabad is protected by the **Asola Wildlife Sanctuary** ⑦.

SEE ALSO ENVIRONMENT, P.37; FORTS, P.57; MONUMENTS, P.81

Below: Lado Sarai flower market, Mehrauli.

In the south of Mehrauli are the colourful tombs of **Jamali Kamali** and the **Hauz-i-Shamsi** reservoir commissioned by Iltutmish in 1230, beside which is the **Jahaz Mahal**, a ruined Lodi pavilion.

The most impressive remains of the now ruined walls of **Qila Lal Kot** lie to the northwest of Mehrauli and the Qutb Minar. The walls of a slightly later fort, the **Qila Rai Pithora**, can be seen just off Aurobindo Marg to the northeast.

SEE ALSO FORTS, P.57; MONUMENTS, P.81; RELIGIOUS SITES, P.111

Gardens, Temples and Museums

Beyond Mehrauli Village, towards the Haryana border and Gurgaon there are a number of other interesting sights. Close to the main Mehrauli-Gurgaon Road, on the western side is the modern **Dada Bari** Jain temple,

near which is the early-Mughal **Madhi Masjid**. Another Jain site can be found a bit further on. The **Ahinsa Sthal** is a monumental statue of the Jain *tirthankara* Mahavir.

Further south is the **Garden of the Five Senses** ③, laid out by Delhi Tourism and opened in 2003. There is a very good restaurant here.

South again are the spectacular modern temples and ashram complexes of **Chattarpur** ④. This is one of the largest temples in India, all carved white marble and huge statues, some of it in slightly dubious taste.

That is not a charge that can be laid against the **Sanskriti Foundation** ⑤ with displays of Indian terracotta and everyday objects and textiles, one of the best in the city.

SEE ALSO MUSEUMS AND GALLERIES, P.91; PARKS AND GARDENS, P.101; RELIGIOUS SITES, P.111

Gurgaon, Noida and Trans-Yamuna

The booming economy of modern India has brought new wealth and purchasing power to the middle class of Delhi, and as the city expands, many have moved out to the satellite cities of Gurgaon and Noida. If you want to see the modern Indian middle class at work and play, visit one of the huge new shopping malls, gawp at the the large steel-and-glass offices of multinational companies, and then try to reconcile this with the grinding poverty of much of the rest of the country.

Above: Western lifestyle magazines on offer in Gurgaon.

Gurgaon

Lying to the south of Mehrauli, the satellite city of **Gurgaon** ① is actually just over the state boundary from Delhi in Haryana. Its proximity to the capital and Delhi Airport has turned it into a boom town, boasting some of the most striking modern architecture to grace the Indian skyline.

This development began in the 1990s when chronic overcrowding in Delhi prompted the Haryana authorities to buy up land and give tax breaks to developers and companies

willing to build or relocate to the city. The employment that accompanied these industries was by and large white-collar and service jobs (read call-centres and IT), making Gurgaon a magnet for the newly powerful Indian middle class.

Transport links between Gurgaon and the centre of Delhi, particularly the airport, were greatly improved by the widening and creation of a toll road along National Highway 8, and are even better now that the Delhi metro extension to the city has been completed.

Accompanying this boom in construction and employment was a greater demand for consumer goods, and soon flashy new shopping malls were springing up all over the place. Gurgaon now has the biggest shopping malls in India. The most impressive examples are the **Ambi Mall** ② at over 1km (⅔ mile) long opened in 2007, while the adjacent, and even bigger, **Mall of India** is due to open in late 2011.

As well as a place to go shopping, Gurgaon can also

Left: the Metropolitan Mall in Gurgaon.

Noida has the same sort of range of malls and places to eat and drink as Gurgaon, but has a particularly lively nightlife that is well worth checking out. Like Gurgaon it is now being connected to the Delhi metro network.

As Delhi continues to push at its borders, the overspill spreads even wider. Now **Ghaziabad** ⑤, on the northeastern border with Uttar Pradesh, is witnessing a similar boom to that which has affected Gurgaon and Noida.

Trans-Yamuna

The area that lies across the Yamuna but is still within the boundaries of Delhi proper is generally referred to as **Trans-Yamuna** ⑥. It is linked to the rest of Delhi by the metro, running from Shahdara through to Kashmere Gate.

Largely a residential area, Trans-Yamuna is also the location of the **Commonwealth Games Athletes' Village**, on the east bank of the river near the **Akshardham Temple** ⑦ *(see box, left)*. The **Yamuna Sports Complex**, to the north, held the archery and table tennis competitions.

SEE ALSO SPORT, P.125

While the satellite cities of Delhi have few sights, Trans-Yamuna has a notable exception, the **Akshardham Temple** complex. Built by the Swaminarayan Foundation, this is not only a temple but, according to the organisers, epitomises 10,000 years of Indian culture in all its breathtaking grandeur, beauty, widsom and bliss. Well worth a look, if only to see the sheer scale of the kitsch on offer *(see also Religious Sites, p.111)*.

make a good place to stay if you do not mind being so far from central Delhi, as there are a number of new luxury hotels here, and it is convenient for the airport. And, of course, the young middle class demand new bars and restaurants, some of which are good to head for if you are staying out this way.

Aside from these attractions, Gurgaon is worth a visit if only to see a completely

different side of India and to check out its sometimes fanciful architecture.
SEE ALSO SHOPPING, P.121, 122

Noida

Also outside the boundary of the National Capital Territory of Delhi, although this time across the Yamuna river in the state of Uttar Pradesh, is the new town of **Noida** ③ (the New Okhla Industrial Development Area). Very similar to Gurgaon, if less self-consciously flash and modern, Noida was set up during the 1970s. Some of the major employers here are companies manufacturing parts for the car industry. Quite a few television serials are also shot here at the **Noida Film City** ④, a large complex of film studios and television companies.

Right: the new metro connects Noida with Delhi.

21

A–Z

In the following section Delhi's attractions and services are organised by theme, under alphabetical headings. Items that link to another theme are cross-referenced. All sights that fall within the area of the atlas section at the end of the book are given a page number and grid reference.

Architecture

Architecturally Delhi is a fascinating city, and there are many gems to be sought out. Its buildings run the gamut from the earliest still extant Islamic monuments in India, through the glories of the tombs and mosques of the Lodis and Mughals, the exceptional planned city of the British empire, to some exemplary modern architecture. Also interesting is the degree to which the city is zoned, with the old Mughal city still very distinct – architecturally and culturally – from those of the British to the north and south, and from the more modern developments further out.

Old Delhi was famed for its *galis* (narrow streets), along which were the high walls of graceful *havelis*. The *haveli* is a large mansion built around a series of courtyards and which is divided into a public area (first courtyard) and private section (second courtyard) for the women of the extended family. While the outside walls may appear austere, the interiors were beautiful and often richly decorated. The real glory of the Delhi *havelis*, though, were their beautiful gardens.

The Early Delhi Sultanates

The earliest monuments of the Delhi Sultanates (and so the earliest still extant examples of architecture in the city) can be seen at the **Qutb Minar Complex** in Mehrauli. Here there is a fusing of Central Asian style with the Hindu architecture of the Rajput kingdoms that had ruled Delhi until that point.

This was partly due to the reusing of pillars and worked stones from Hindu temples, but also local builders stuck to the arches that they were

used to, not those used elsewhere in the Islamic world (although the radiating arch soon made its entry in India). The Qutb Minar Complex also sees the introduction of the dome (as on the tomb of Iltutmish) and the minaret (the Qutb Minar itself), as well as the use of calligraphy and geometric patterning as decoration on the minaret's façade.

Tombs and fortifications tended to be massively built of rubble and stone, with sloping rather than vertical

walls, as can be seen in **Tughlaqabad**.

SEE ALSO FORTS, P.57; MONUMENTS, P.82

The Lodis and Sayyids

By the time of the rule of the Lodis and Sayyids in Delhi during the 15th and 16th centuries, Islamic architecture had firmly established itself in the city. The use of the dome had become ubiquitous on tombs and had progressed from the shallow domes seen on early Sultanate architecture to the

Left: the *charbagh* layout of Safdarjang's Tomb.

dome is on a much more intimate and human scale.

Mughal royal monuments also made extensive use of *pietra dura*, the inlay of semi-precious stones, and intially artisans were brought across from Italy to pass on their skills and knowledge.

Delhi is the location of one of the great examples of Mughal town planning, the city of **Shahjahanabad** (or Old Delhi). With the main palace (the **Lal Qila**) and central place of worship (the **Jama Masjid**) to the east, the city was conceived around two axes, Chandni Chowk and the present-day Netaji Subhash Marg, and the town was divided into wards, separated by roads, each with a sense of neighbourhood based on shared ties of kinship or occupation. The whole city was surrounded by substantial walls, punctuated at regular intervals by impressive gateways, some of which are still standing.

SEE ALSO FORTS, P.54; MONUMENTS, P.78, 80; RELIGIONS AND RELIGIOUS SITES, P.107

British Delhi

The first architectural impact of the arrival of the British

Left: the once elegant city of Old Delhi is now run-down.

more bulbous form that was to be perfected by the Mughals. Tombs became more delicate in their construction, developing the octagonal form to great effect in the monuments of **Lodi Gardens**. By this time a languge of Indo-Islamic architecture, especially in the building of tombs, had become established, with features such as *chatris* (open kiosks), minarets and double-arched entrance ways topped with a dome.

SEE ALSO MONUMENTS, P.79; PARKS AND GARDENS, P.100

Mughal Delhi

These features were all to be refined and brought to a greater sense of perfection by the Mughals. Their great innovation was the *charbagh* layout of the 'garden tomb'. In this, seen to its best advantage in the tombs of **Humayun** and **Safdarjang**,

the tomb is placed at the centre of a square garden compound, which itself is subdivided into squares through the means of paths and water features. This was a development of Central Asian garden design that the Mughal rulers brought with them to India.

The dome was also developed with the concept of the double dome. In this a smaller dome is set within the much larger external one. Thus the outside gives an impression of power and nobility, while the internal

Right: one of Lutyens's and Baker's New Delhi bungalows.

25

Left: the stupa-inspired dome of Rashtrapati Bahvan behind the soaring Jaipur Column.

Metcalfe House is, if anything, finer, with distinctly Indo-Islamic influence on the façade and in the arched windows and colonnades.

After 1857, however, such experiments were to cease, and much of the architecture that followed was either neo-classical, as in the Old Secretariat bulding, or neo-Gothic, as shown by the **Mutiny Memorial**.

Once, however, the decision was taken in 1911 to move the capital of India back to Delhi and to build a totally new city as the centre of the administration, things were to change again and that was down to one man – Edwin Lutyens.

SEE ALSO MONUMENTS, P.77; RELIGIONS AND RELIGIOUS SITES, P.108

LUTYENS AND BAKER

Born in London in 1869, Edwin Landseer Lutyens was known principally for his work on English country houses prior to his appointment as chief architect of New Delhi. Lutyens chose as his associate Herbert Baker, with whom he had collaborated in South Africa. They decided that Lutyens would be responsible for the overall concept, the **Viceroy's House** and the **War Memorial**, while Baker would design the administrative buidings and the legislative assembly.

There was great pressure on the two men to produce a synthesis of British and Indian architectural styles, but after a tour of the country Lutyens wrote, 'Personally, I

Hindu temples *(mandir)* are built with beams and feature low ceilings, narrow doorways and hundreds of pillars, unlike the Indian mosques *(masjid)*, which have spacious interiors reflecting the introduction of the true arch in Muslim architecture. Hindu temple architecture is highly symbolic – a cosmology in miniature planned to entice a particular deity back to visit a place. The sacred sanctum, where the image of the presiding deity resides in a darkened chamber, is almost always square-shaped and must be orientated towards one of the cardinal points. A towering roof structure, a *shikhara*, soars above the inner sanctum to make the holy place visible from a distance.

was to the north of the Old City of Shahjahanabad, in what became known as the **Civil Lines**. Bringing with them 19th-century European ideas on architecture, they began to erect buildings that would not have looked out of place in Britain. Notable among these are **St James's Church** or the classical façade added to the Mughal palace of **Dara Shikoh**.

Not all British architecture, however, was immune from the influence of the buildings that surrounded it. Two important buildings of the first half of the 19th century show distinct Indian features. **William Fraser's House,** close by St James's Church, sports a large dome that at least makes a nod to the domed buildings to the south in Old Delhi. The

Right: the India Habitat Centre.

do not believe there is any real Indian architecture, or any great tradition,' while Baker agreed: Hindu architecture was 'grotesque, meaningless carving' and Mughal 'masses of brick covered with decoration'. Both agreed that the new city must be 'neither Indian nor English nor Roman, but Imperial', that it must be spacious and symmetrical, in sharp contrast with the organic feel of Old Delhi, and must, above all, symbolise the system and order that the British administration felt it had imposed upon the country.

It is perhaps surprising, then, that so many elements of Indian design made it onto their buildings, such as *chatris*, *chajjas* (stone cornices) and *jalis* (carved screens), as well as symbols like lotuses and bells.

Indeed, Lutyens's *magnum opus*, **Rashtrapati Bhavan**, sports a vast copper dome encircled by a stone railing, clearly inspired by the Buddhist stupa at Sanchi. At the centre of the court in front of the building he placed another imperial symbol, but

one firmly in an Indian tradition, the Jaipur Column. Commemorative pillars had long been used by Indian rulers, from Ashoka to the Qutb Minar, and the 43.5-m (143-ft) column culminates brilliantly in a bronze Indian lotus, crowned with a crystal star.

Lutyens's masterplan is ingenious, a garden city with wide, straight vistas, low buildings (hence the predominance of bungalows) and plenty of trees and parks. The whole was set out on a vast hexagonal grid that centred around the long, straight road of Kingsway, now Rajpath. If you stand on Raisina Hill just outside the iron grille of Rashtrapati Bhavan and look down, the perfect symmetry of Lutyens's plan is immediately evident.

Modern Delhi

The 'empire on which the sun will never set' was not, of course, destined to last, and after Independence Lutyens's and Baker's city was inherited by the new rulers. Pushed for cash and having pressing priorites of industrial development, little of archi-

tectural worth was produced in the years immediately after Independence, one exception being the Supreme Court building, nicely in tune with its surroundings, built by the Central Public Works Department in 1958.

A change of direction came with the Modernist **India International Centre** building in 1962, designed by J.A. Stein. He was also responsible for the later **India Habitat Centre** (1994), one of the most successful modern buildings in the city with its light and airy interior courtyards.

One architect who has made his mark on the city is the Indian Charles Correa. His **Life Insurance of India Building** (known as Jeevan Bharati Bhavan) on Connaught Place with its reflective glass façade drew much comment when first built, but perhaps more successful is his elegant **British Council Building** on Kasturba Gandhi Marg. Mention should also be made of the **Asian Games Village** (1982) by Raj Rewal that takes its inspiration from vernacular Indian urban housing.

Cafés and Bars

Delhi offers quite a mixture in the sitting, drinking and dancing stakes – from traditional coffee shops serving the frothy South Indian real deal and tasty fried snacks, to chains catering to latte-swilling students and young executives, to trendy designer bars serving up sophisticated cocktails. There is a good concentration of all these different places, as you might expect, around Connaught Place, but do not neglect the luxury hotels and the colonies of South Delhi with some of the best places in the city. This is also one area where Gurgaon and Noida score highly with a good concentration of bars.

Connaught Place

@Live

K12, Outer Circle, Connaught Place; tel: 4356 0008; daily 12.30pm–midnight; metro: Rajiv Chowk; map p.137 C4

Run by the owners of Q'BA, this has more the feel of a down-to-earth drinking place than its sister establishment, albeit with the same great sense of design. As well as live music every night there is a great cocktail list to wade your way through.

1911

Hotel Imperial, 1 Janpath; tel: 2334 1234; daily 11.30am–12.45am; metro: Rajiv Chowk; map p.137 C4

The bar at the Imperial is sheer class (in the 'upper' sense). Quiet and refined with a huge selection of drinks, the outside seating overlooking the manicured lawns might well be the best place in the city to have your sundowner of a pink gin. Make sure you have your posh togs on.

Agni

The Park, 15 Sansad Marg; tel: 2374 3000; daily 24 hours; metro: Rajiv Chowk; map p.137 C4

Above: cocktails at Q'BA.

Given the name, it is appropriate that The Park's DJ bar has a fire theme, all oranges and reds. Given that it's in one of Delhi's top design hotels you would expect it to be stylish, and it is. With a good selection of cocktails, it's a good choice for a chic night out.

Coffee Home

Baba Kharak Singh Marg, opposite the Hanuman Mandir; tel: 2336 3813; daily 11am– 8pm; metro: Rajiv Chowk; map p.137 C4

Set up by the government and modelled on the coop-

India's answer to Starbucks is the phenomenally popular chain **Barista**. Its first coffee shop opened in 2000, in Delhi, and now there are over 40 branches throughout the city (for a full list see www.barista.co.in), some of them in Corner bookshops. The coffee and snacks are on a par with Starbucks, along the lines of blueberry muffins and grande skinny vanilla lattes; if that's your thing then Barista will feel like a home from home.

ative coffee houses of South India, this is not the most glamorous location in the capital, but it does have a certain charm and honesty that goes to show what India is in danger of losing as it throws itself headlong into international corporate chic. Good coffee and excellent South Indian snacks (*dosas* and *vada*) are served on concrete benches and tables.

Q'BA

E42–43, Connaught Place; tel: 4151 2888; daily noon–12.30am; metro: Rajiv Chowk; map p.137 C4

Left: @Live in CP.

Although primarily listed here as a restaurant this designed-to-within-an-inch-of-its-life space is also great for a drink and dance, especially later on when the DJs get going in earnest. Not quiet or laid-back, but it can be a lot of fun.
SEE ALSO RESTAURANTS, P.114

Rajpath and Chanakyapuri

Aura
The Claridges, 12 Aurangzeb Road; tel: 4133 5133; 4pm–1am; metro: Udyog Bhavan; map p.137 C2
The vodka bar at The Claridges *(see p.62)* is suitably hard-edged to go with the raw spirit. Lots of steel, glass and loud music accompany your trip through the over 60 different vodkas on offer. There is an impressive cocktail list – seemingly designed to get as much flavourless spirit inside you as possible – shaken and stirred by the well-trained bar staff.

F Bar and Lounge
The Ashok Hotel, 50B Chanakyapuri; tel: 2611 0101; daily noon–1am; metro: Dhaula Kuan; map p.136 B1

One of the trendier places in town, which caused quite a stir when it first opened, this is a large but super-stylish and comfortable space, arranged over two floors and with a spectacular terrace overlooking Connaught Place. The food is OK, but Q'BA is best used for a classy drink and for Delhi star-spotting.

Spirit
E34, Connaught Place; tel: 4101 7006; daily noon–midnight; metro: Rajiv Chowk; map p.137 C4
This classy bar/restaurant has some decent Middle Eastern and Mediterranean food (the Indian dishes are not up to scratch). It also has a better wine list than most, and tends to play music at a volume low enough that conversation remains a possibility, a bit of a rarity in Delhi.

United Coffee House
E15 Connaught Place; tel: 2341 1697; daily 10am–11.30pm; metro: Rajiv Chowk; map p.137 C4

The food and drinks are not the real attraction here (pretty standard fare); it is the nicely dated décor and ambience that set this place apart. A bit of an old travellers' haunt – you won't find any of Delhi's young movers and shakers here – but still worth dropping in for a coffee or beer if you are in the area.

Veda
H26–27, Connaught Place; tel: 4151 3535; daily noon–11.30pm; metro: Rajiv Chowk; map p.137 C4

Right: meeting up at Q'BA.

While you may not wish to stay at the huge pile that is the Ashok, it is worth a visit to gawp at the Bentley showroom, visit the spa and have a drink at the FTV-sponsored fashion-themed cocktail bar. Weird and wonderful concoctions are dished up amidst the glittery lights, attracting a fairly laid-back crowd.

Ricks
Taj Mahal, 1 Mansingh Road; tel: 2302 6162; daily 12.30pm–1am; metro: Central Secretariat; map p.137 D2

The best cocktails in the city? Probably. They have a huge list of drinks here, from Martinis and sours to ones you have never heard of. Relaxed but with an upmarket feel, the subdued décor makes this a good place for a quiet drink. The food on offer, a mix of American and Southeast Asian dishes, is pretty good as well.

Sevilla
The Claridges, 12 Aurangzeb Road; tel: 4133 5133; Wed–Mon 7.30pm–12.30am; metro: Central Secretariat; map p.137 C2

The second of the two great bars at The Claridges is ostensibly Spanish-themed, but with food that ranges from one end of the Mediter-

ranean to the other. It is pretty good, as are the drinks (which include, of course, sangria) but it is the ambience that is a real winner; outdoors in the beautiful garden and sitting in discrete tented enclosures – bliss.

Lodi Gardens and Nizamuddin
Café Turtle
Full Circle Bookshop, 2nd floor, 23, Middle Lane, Khan Market; tel: 2465 5641; daily 10am–9.30pm; metro: Khan Market; map p.137 D2

There's a laid-back, if slightly cramped, feel to this innovative bookshop café. As well as a few Indian-inspired items, there are good pasta dishes and salads, but the cakes are even better. There are also now branches at N16, Greater Kailash I and 8 Nizamuddin East Market.

SEE ALSO LITERATURE AND THEATRE, P.73

Choko la
36 Khan Market; tel: 4175 7570; daily 8am–11pm; metro: Khan Market; map p.137 D2

Like many places in Khan Market, the pleasantly chic modern interior does not reveal itself until you climb the stairs. Excellent cakes and chocolates, along with

coffee and fresh juices, can be consumed in the light, airy space. The top-floor balcony is particularly pleasant.

The Tapas Lounge
Aman Hotel, Lodi Road; tel: 4363 3333; daily noon–1am; metro: JL Nehru Stadium; map p.137 D2

Extremely classy bar, offering all manner of authentic tapas to a discerning clientele – not cheap, but the best of its type in town.

South Delhi
Ai
Second Floor, MGF Metropolitan Mall, Saket; tel: 4065 4567; daily 12pm–12am; metro: Saket; map p.139 C1

One of the hippest joints in Delhi, particularly popular with the younger ex-pat set. The sushi is superb, if painfully pricey, but it's as the night gets later that this place comes alive, morphing into a full-on disco by closing time.

Beer Café
Second Floor, Ambience Mall, Nelson Mandela Marg, Vasant Kunj; tel: 4087 0509; daily noon–midnight; metro: Hauz Khas; map p.138 A2

Novel newcomer to Delhi's bar scene, the USP here is

Right: at Mannekin.

Left: Café Turtle, Khan Market.

the self-service beer towers at every table, delivering ice-cold beer at the swipe of a card. There's also an extremely well-stocked bar, offering over 30 international varieties, in a vibrant interior. Well worth a try.

The Flipside
7 Hauz Khas Village; tel: 2651 6341; Wed-Mon 10am–8pm, metro: Haus Khaz; map p.138 B3
Funky new café offering great coffee, cakes, pizzas and crepes, as well as always delicious daily specials. The vibe is relaxed, with a fresher soundtrack than Delhi is used to. Highly recommended.

Kylin
24 Basant Lok, Vasant Vihar; tel: 4166 9778; daily noon–12.30am; metro: Haus Khaz; map p.138 A3
Kylin is a bit of a find, even if it is off the beaten track for most visitors. Laid-back and quietly chic, this bar is great for a drink or for the East Asian food on offer. It is advisable to phone ahead to book a table to guarantee getting in.

Le Café
N1, N Block Market, Greater Kailash I; tel: 4173 1035; daily 11am–10pm; metro: East of Kailash; map p.139 D3
Run by the people behind Diva, this Italian-style café is

Barista was not the first Indian coffee house to recognise the demand for a pleasant space serving decent coffee: that honour belongs to the Bangalore-based chain **Café Coffee Day**, which started in 1996. Now it is the most widespread franchise of cafés in India, serving very good coffee (by common consent better than at Barista). You can't miss it as there are over 80 branches in Delhi, all of which can be found on their website (www.cafe coffeeday.com).

a great place for a drink or a light meal (mostly Italian snacks and East Asian dishes). Nicely thought out, the pleasant space tempts you to linger over your coffee, which, as befits an Italian-inspired café, is some of the best in Delhi.

Mannekin
Kasbah, N2 Market, Greater Kailash I; tel: 4163 5000; daily noon–11.30pm; metro: East of Kailash; map p.139 D3
Part of the Kasbah restaurant complex, Mannekin is a good place for a quiet drink, at least early on before the DJ gets going. Comfy and not as in-your-face as some places, it draws in a mixed crowd who are looking more for a chat and to pick at the decent food on offer than for

a wild night on the tiles.
SEE ALSO RESTAURANTS, P.117

Moksha
8 Community Centre, New Friends Colony; tel: 4167 2777; daily 12.30–3pm, 7.30pm–midnight; metro: Lajpat Nagar
One of a cluster of bars that have opened up in Friends Colony, and this one is perfectly good for a drink if you are in the area, and especially known for its good wine list. It is popular among a wide range of South Delhiites and has the occasional live band on.

Mystique Heights
1st and 2nd Floor, 15 Community Centre, New Friends Colony; tel: 5132 8184; daily noon–1am; metro: Lajpat Nagar
Another Friends Colony bar that is perhaps not necessarily worth a special trip out from the centre, but a good place for a relaxing drink if you are in the area. Like Moksha *(above)*, it is very popular locally and packs in the crowds later on once the DJ starts cranking the music up.

Onyx
The Manor, 77 Friends Colony West; tel: 2692 5151; daily 11.30am–11.30pm; metro: Lajpat Nagar
The bar at The Manor *(see p.66)* is a quietly classy affair, more upmarket than some of the other bars in

the area, and is generally used by the hotel guests or locals looking for a low-key place to chill out. It looks out on the lovely gardens and has some excellent cocktails as well as tasty North Indian food.

Opus Lounge
47 Basant Lok, Vasant Vihar; tel: 6569 1265; daily noon–1am; metro: Haus Khaz; map p.138 A3

Like the Kylin *(see p.31),* this is another good place for a drink out in Vasant Vihar. The Opus Lounge is a bit livelier than the Kylin and the menu more varied (taking in European and East Asian dishes). Quiet, small and attractive, it is a good place to go with a group of friends to eat, drink and listen to some music.

Polo Lounge
Hyatt Regency, Bhikaiji Cama Place, Ring Road; tel: 2679 1234; daily 11am–1am; map p.138 B4

The bar at the Hyatt *(see p.66)* seems at first to be a bit fuddy-duddy, but it is worth moving beyond the faux-gentlemen's-club décor to get at the cocktails on offer. Not the place to ask for a pomegranate daiquiri

or kumquat martini, in keeping with the ambience the drinks tend to be based on cognac, champagne and whisky and are intended for savouring.

Shalom
N18, Greater Kailash I; tel: 4163 2280; daily 12.30–3.30pm, 7.30pm–1am; metro: East of Kailash; map p.139 D3

One of Delhi's best-known and most popular bars, for good reason. Its popularity means it is best to book in advance, but once you are there the quietly chic interior is the perfect place to sup a few of its top-class cocktails. It is also known for its Mediterranean food, which is tasty enough to order without the need to soak up some alcohol. A new branch of the bar has opened in Vasant Vihar, adding to that area's clutch of good places to eat and drink.

Urban Pind
N4, Greater Kailash I; tel: 3251 5656; daily 1pm–1am; metro: East of Kailash; map p.139 D3

This Khajaraho-themed lounge bar/restaurant is popular with ex-pats, particularly the diplomatic set, and is decent enough for a drink and a night out if you can stand the company. The

Indian and Italian-inspired snacks are tasty, but the cocktails are better.

Mehrauli and Tughlaqabad

Bar SaVanh
Qutb Golf Course, Aurobindo Marg, Lado Sarai; tel: 2952 3330; daily noon–3.30pm, 7pm–12.30am; metro: Qutab Minar; map p.138 C1

Attached to the excellent **IndoChine** is this equally good lounge bar, serving inventive and naughtily named cocktails. Currently one of the favourites with Delhi's 'it' crowd, it is a good place to see and be seen.
SEE ALSO RESTAURANTS, P.119

Buzz
2nd Floor, 17 Commercial Centre, Saket; tel: 2956 3501; daily 12.30pm–midnight; metro: Saket; map p.138 C1

This buzzy and trendy bar is popular with those looking for a lively night of boozing and dancing but in a tasteful space. Packed with a wide range of people, it's friendly and good for a night of little conversation and even less thinking. There is a branch at DLF City in Gurgaon.

Kuki

E7, Community Centre, LSC
Masjid Moth, Greater Kailash II;
tel: 2922 5241; daily 6pm–1am;
metro: Kalkaji Mandirmap; p.139
E2

One of the newer places in
town, this large club and bar
has been attracting the
young and beautiful of Delhi
since it opened. A good
place for a night out dancing,
but it does have a steepish
entrance charge (women get
in free on Wednesdays).
Good finger food and the
usual dangerous cocktails
are on offer.

Smoke House Grill

2 VIPPS Centre, LSC Masjid Moth,
Greater Kailash II; tel: 4143
5530; daily 12.30–3.30pm,
7.30pm–1am; metro: Kalkaji
Mandir; map p.139 E2

Like Veda (see p.30), the
Smoke House Grill is first and
foremost a good place to eat,
but it has gained a city-wide
reputation for its cocktails,
which include some of the
tastiest and most unusual
creations to be had in the city.

Tabula Rasa

4th Floor, Square One Mall, Saket;
tel: 2956 2666; daily noon–1am;
metro: Saket; map p.138 C1

One of the best places for a
drink in South Delhi, Tabula
Rasa has a beautifully
designed interior, with water
features. Generally a restful
place to lie back with a cocktail in hand, it livens up at the
weekend, when a DJ packs
the dance floor.

Gurgaon and Noida

The Deck

3rd Floor, 301–302 Sahara Mall,
Mehrauli–Gurgaon Road, Gurgaon; tel: 0124-404 8031; daily
8.30pm–1am; metro: Gurgaon

This is priimarily a dance
club, playing a good mixture
of Bollywood tracks and hip-
hop. One of the better places
in Gurgaon, and the drinks
are more straightforward than
in some other bars.

Elevate

6th Floor, L1 Centre Stage Mall,
Sector 18, Noida; tel: 0120-436
4611; Fri–Sat 10pm–4am;
metro: Noida Sector 18

This weekends-only club in
Noida is one of the best in
Delhi, pulling in the crowds
from across the city. A wide
range of music is played
here, depending on which DJ
is in residence. The space is
the largest in India, and the
drinks are pretty reasonable.

Fluid

Hotel Mosaic, C-1 Sector 18,
Noida; tel: 0120-402 5000; daily
2–11pm; metro: Noida Sector 18

A bit far-flung, but one of the
best and most popular DJ
bars in the city. All very chic –
water-themed like Aqua at
The Park – with places to
lounge around as well as a
dance floor. The cocktail and
wine lists are particularly
impressive.

Mojo

CS-211, DLF City Centre,
Mehrauli–Gurgaon Road,
Gurgaon; tel: 0124-257 5695;
daily noon–2am; metro:
Gurgaon

Everything you might want
under one roof, a bar/restau-
rant and a club space. Good
for drinking given the range
of high-quality booze on
offer, and the DJs manage to
get a good vibe going most
nights. The food is an OK-ish
international mix.

Peppers

The Bristol Hotel, DLF Qutb
Enclave Phase I, Gurgaon;
tel: 0124-235 6030; daily
9.30pm–4am; metro: Gurgaon

Gurgaon seems to be
Delhi's club centre at present, with another good place
in operation. The drinks at
Peppers are fairly straightforward and the food basic
(and best avoided), but this
is a great place for a night
out dancing.

> While Delhi might be developing
> an active bar and drinking
> scene, remember that this is
> still very much a minority activ-
> ity, restricted in general to the
> young middle class, and will be
> frowned on by many Indians.
> Also, Delhi is not necessarily a
> safe place for women who have
> drunk too much – make sure
> you can get back to where you
> are staying safely. Also bear in
> mind that the legal minimum
> age for drinking in Delhi is – in
> theory at least – 25, although
> that is soon to be dropped to 21.

Left: Urban Pind.

Children

Delhi is a surprisingly easy place to bring children, and in which to keep them amused. In general you will find that Indians love children, and there will be very few places (barring, of course, bars and clubs) where they will not be welcome. Do be aware that the summer heat can be very difficult for young children and babies, and it is essential that they keep hydrated and out of the fierce Indian sun. Travelling with small children is now much easier as disposable nappies are widely available, as are specialist (and probably familiar) brands of formula milk and baby food.

What to Do

The range of activities to keep the kids amused in Delhi will largely depend on the time of year, and some of the options may be ruled out by the heat during the summer.

Delhi has a number of parks, most of which have some sort of children's playground, but easily the pick of the bunch is the **Children's Park at India Gate**, with more swings and slides than the rest of the parks put together. **The Garden of the Five Senses** is another place that should keep children entertained for a while, and **Lodi Gardens** in particular is a good place for kids to run around and let off some

steam; close to Purana Qila, east of India Gate, there is a boating lake which might also appeal to younger visitors. Out on the Delhi-Gurgaon border is the **Fun'n'Food Village**, an amusement complex with swimming and rides.

Once it gets really hot there are a few museums that are good for kids. One of them is the **National Science Centre Museum**, part of the Pragati Maidan complex east of India Gate, which has a fair number of push-button, interactive displays, as well as a walk-through dinosaur jungle. **Shankar's International Dolls Museum**, part of the Nehru House complex at 4 Bahadur Shah Zafar Marg, is

an absolute doll fest, with no fewer than 6,500 of them from all over the world.

The **National Rail Museum** is a good place to take children, and they will especially enjoy riding around the grounds on the monorail. Others that might be worth a visit include the **National Museum of Natural History** and the **Planetarium at the Nehru Museum**.

Another possibility is the **Children's Riding Club** (tel: 2301 2265) just behind Safdarjang's Tomb, where kids can have a ride around a paddock on some suitably small ponies, and run round the small farm next door. About the best option when the weather is too hot to be outdoors is Buddies Planet in Ansal Plaza shopping centre on Khel Gaon Marg. It's an indoor play area boasting slides and ball pools, but best of all, it's air-conditioned.

Visit www.theplayground delhi.com for other ideas on kid-friendly activities.

Left: a brightly painted engine at the Rail Museum.

Left: wooden toys for sale at Dilli Haat, *see p.123.*

grounds of the Nehru Memorial Museum has shows for kids in English at 11.30am and 3pm.
SEE ALSO MUSEUMS AND GALLERIES, P.88

National Rail Museum
Chanakyapuri; tel: 2688 1816; www.nrm.indianrailways.gov.in; Tue–Sun Oct–Mar 9.30am–1pm, 1.30–5.30pm, Apr–Sept 9.30am–1pm, 1.30–7.30pm; entrance charge; metro: Race Course; map p.136 B1
SEE ALSO MUSEUMS AND GALLERIES, P.89

National Science Centre Museum
Near Gate 1, Pragati Maidan, Bhairon Road; tel: 2337 1297; www.nscdelhi.org; daily 10am–5.30pm; entrance charge; metro: Pragati Maidan; map p.137 E3
SEE ALSO MUSEUMS AND GALLERIES, P.89

Gurgaon

Fun'n'Food Village
Old Delhi–Gurgaon Road, Kapashera; tel: 4326 0000; www.funnfood.com; summer: 10am–10pm, winter: 10am–8pm; entrance charge; metro: IFFCO Chowk; This adventure park has rides, pools and water slides.

Zoos are controversial places at the best of times, and Indian zoos in particular more resemble concentration camps and torture chambers than viable habitats for their hapless inmates. Although **Delhi Zoo** (Purana Qila; tel: 2461 9825; daily summer 9am–7pm, winter 9.30am–5.30pm; entrance charge) is said to be one of the better ones in the country, with largish enclosures, those of a sensitive disposition (or with regard for animal welfare) might wish to give it a miss. For further information visit www.petaindia.com, www.aapn.org and www.zoocheck.com.

SEE ALSO PARKS AND GARDENS P.100, 101

Connaught Place

National Museum of Natural History
FICCI Museum Building, Barakhamba Road; tel: 2331 4849; www.nmnh.nic.in; Tue–Sun 10am–5pm; entrance charge; metro: Mandi House; map p.137 D4
SEE ALSO MUSEUMS AND GALLERIES, P.84

Shankar's International Dolls Museum
Nehru House, 4 Bahadur Shah Zafar Marg; tel: 2331 6970; www.childrensbooktrust.com; Tue–Sun 10am–6pm; entrance charge; metro: Pragati Maidan; map p.135 D1
SEE ALSO MUSEUMS AND GALLERIES, P.85

Old Delhi and Raj Ghat

National Children's Museum
Bal Bhavan, 1 Kotla Marg; tel: 2323 2672; www.national balbhavan.nic.in; Tue–Sat 9am–5.30pm; entrance charge; metro: Barakhamba Road; map p.135 D1
SEE ALSO MUSEUMS AND GALLERIES, P.86

Rajpath and Chanakyapuri

Jawaharlal Nehru Memorial Museum
Teen Murti Bhavan, Teen Murti Marg; tel: 2301 7587; www.nehrumemorial.com; Tue–Sun 10am–3pm; free; metro: Udyog Bhavan; map p.136 B2
The Planetarium in the

Right: balls and balloons in Lodi Gardens.

35

Environment

Like any large, developing city, Delhi faces considerable environmental challenges. There is a lack of power, water and sanitation for its rapidly growing population, the city streets are increasingly congested as car ownership rockets among the newly wealthy middle class, and developers try to encroach on yet more of the city's green spaces. All is not doom and gloom, however: the city has one of the more forward-thinking governments in India and has already converted its public transport to run on CNG, built a brand new metro system and is now trying to eliminate plastic bags.

Environmental Issues

With a population of over 18 million and more than 1.6 million cars on its streets, Delhi is a city with more than a few environmental problems on its hands. In common with all Indian cities, one of the greatest difficulties it faces is in providing sanitation and efficient water treatment for its population, and while this seems to be adequate for most of the middle-class colonies, for the vast majority of the city's inhabitants it is poor, if not non-existent.

As well as problems of shortages of water, – especially in the summer – and

As most visitors from abroad fly into Delhi, they too are having an environmental impact. Air travel produces a huge amount of carbon dioxide and is a significant contributor to climate change. One way of partially limiting the damage is to 'offset' the carbon emissions. In the UK, travellers can log on to www.climatecare.org, or in the US www.sustainabletravel international.org.

sanitation, Delhi is increasingly power-hungry. This comes to a head in the summer, when the increase in demand for power from air-conditioning units, plus generally less power from hydroelectric sources, contributes to shortages and black-outs, referred to as 'load shedding'.

Delhi is now the most popular and desirable place in India to live, and as such it attacts new inhabitants on a daily basis. This in turn puts pressure on the city's infrastructure, and the increasingly crowded streets become even more congested. With all these new arrivals, developers illegally encroach on public and protected land, taking over more and more of the city's green spaces.

To be fair, the city government has taken some steps to try to counter these problems (to have a look at the current campaigns it is running, visit www.environment. delhigovt.nic.in). The Delhi government destroyed a large number of illegal buildings (albeit after being forced to by the Supreme Court) and in

Above: a flowering tree in a Delhi park.

2001 switched all its public transport – buses and auto rickshaws – to run off compressed natural gas (CNG is a common sign on the city's buses and green-painted autos). The latter measure made huge improvements to Delhi's air quality.

However, those improvements are now being threatened by the huge rise in private car ownership in the city. A car is now a must-have for any self-respecting member of Delhi's middle class, and as the numbers on the roads continue to increase, not only do the traffic jams,

Left: monkeys can often be spotted in Delhi.

of town, just past Gurgaon, is Sultanpur Bird Sanctuary – particularly impressive in the winter months.

For more information on birdwatching and wildlife in Delhi, contact:

Delhi Bird, the Northern Indian Bird Network
C1/503, Mayfair Tower, Eros Garden, Faridabad, Haryana; tel: 981-000 8625; www. delhibird.net

SEE ALSO PARKS AND GARDENS, P.100

FURTHER READING
A Book of Indian Birds, by **Salim Ali** (Bombay Natural History Society, 2002). Thirteenth revised edition of the classic guide to Indian birds, suitable for novice and experienced birdwatchers.
Pocket Guide to the Birds of the Indian Subcontinent, by **Richard Grimmett, Carol Inskipp and Tim Inskipp** (New Delhi, 1999). Illustrated guide for keen ornithologists, in a handy size.
This Fissured Land, by **Madhav Gadgil and Ramachandra Guha** (Oxford University Press, 1993). Searching and thought-provoking ecological history of South Asia.

congestion and accidents rise, but the gains in air quality made over recent years are now being pushed back.

More hope lies in the excellent progress being made by the city's new metro system. Fast, clean and efficient, as the journey time by car begins to increase along with the congestion, along many routes the metro is now the most convenient way to travel through the city.

A lesser problem, although one that has been taxing the authorities for a number of years, are the cows that wander around Delhi's streets. A sacred animal to the Hindus, many are allowed to roam at will. Apart from the animal welfare aspect of having the creatures trying to survive in an urban environment, the cows clog up the roads and cause accidents (you can be imprisoned for accidently injuring a cow and so people swerve to avoid them, and occasionally hit something else or lose control of their bike or car). The authorities have been ordered to clear them from the roads many times, but with over

2,300 illegal dairies in the city and the risk of wounding religious sensibilities, they are facing an uphill struggle.

Wildlife

While Delhi might seem like a big city with little space for people, let alone wildlife, visitors might be surprised to learn that it has one of the highest species counts of birds of any city in the world. Wildlife along the **Central Ridge** including langur monkeys, jackals, owls, kites, pythons and cobras, still manages to hold on to its place in the city's ecosystem, even if it is finding it increasingly hard to do so.

To the south of the city, just beyond Tughlaqabad, is the **Asola Wildlife Sanctuary**. Established in 1992, it covers around 28 sq km (11 sq miles), and provides a habitat for small mammals, reptiles and birds, including mongoose, jungle cats and monitor lizards. Slightly further out

Right: a sign of the times, Delhi even has its own Bentley showroom.

37

Essentials

In general, Delhi is an easy city to navigate, and most visitors should encounter few problems other than the occasional unwanted attention from hawkers and beggers. Delhi's climate can be quite extreme: freezing cold at times in the winter, while during the summer it is best if you stay out of the blazing sun and make sure that you stay hydrated by drinking lots of water. The infamous 'Delhi belly' is easy to avoid as long as you take simple precautions, and if you do need help or advice Delhiites are in general extremely friendly and helpful, so do not be afraid to ask.

Begging

Visitors to Delhi will encounter people asking for alms, especially around Connaught Place and at traffic lights. Many of them are physically disabled and they have few other options for survival. Small amounts of money (up to about Rs 10) will be gratefully received and will generally be helping someone out. Try to give discreetly or you might attract unwanted attention. If you are unsure about whether to give or not, it is fine simply to follow what other people around you are doing.

Climate

Delhi has one of the world's more wildly fluctuating climates. While May and June can be unbearably hot, with mid-40s°C (around 113°F) the norm, winters can be surprisingly cold – night-time temperatures can get down to freezing point, and the cold air produces fog which often lingers until mid-morning. Humidity remains low for most of the year, with only the build-up to the monsoon

Above: opening times can be a little erratic in Delhi.

and the rainy season (July–Sept) itself feeling especially humid. The most pleasant times to visit are from October to December and mid-February to mid-March, when nights are cool enough to sleep without air-conditioning or a fan, but days are still bright and sunny.

Clothing

What you bring to wear will be largely dictated by the timing of your visit. The pronounced difference in day- and night-time temperatures from late October to mid-March means that you'll need both light and warm clothes, while from mid-March to October you'll rarely need long sleeves, even at night. Indians tend to dress more formally than their counterparts in the West, while women generally cover up more. Attitudes are beginning to change, however, with the younger generation starting to adopt the default Western fashion of the jeans and T-shirt variety. While women will feel comfortable dressing as they would at home in the more salubrious South Delhi neighbourhoods, they should definitely be careful to cover up elsewhere, taking particular care in Old Delhi and other Muslim areas.

Crime and Safety

While Delhi generally feels a safe place to be, women on their own should take extra care. The pernicious male adolescent pastime of 'Eve-teasing', which involves the stroking or even grabbing of female body parts, while rarely done with any serious intent, is obviously a cause for concern. Muggings are extremely rare, although

Left: make sure to obey rules.

Embassies and High Commissions

Australian High Commission: 1-50G Shanti Path, Chanakyapuri; tel: 5139 9900; www.india.embassy.gov.au; map p.136 B1

British High Commission: Shanti Path, Chanakyapuri; tel: 2687 2161; www.ukinindia. fco.gov.uk/en; map p.136 B1

Canadian High Commission: 7–8 Shanti Path, Chanakyapuri; tel: 4178 2000; www.india.gc.ca; map p.136 B1

Irish Embassy: 13 Jor Bagh; tel: 2462 6733; www.irelandinindia .com; map p.137 D1

New Zealand High Commission: 50N Nyaya Marg, Chanakyapuri; tel: 4688 3170; www. nzembassy.com/india; map p.136 B2

US Embassy: Shanti Path, Chanakyapuri; tel: 2419 8000; www.newdelhi.usembassy.gov; map p.136 B1

Gay and Lesbian Travellers

Homosexuality is no longer illegal in India, and increasingly accepted, particularly among the urban young. Having said that, there are few specifically gay venues in Delhi, few completely 'out' Indians and few openly gay relationships among Indians. Owing to this

Below: no need to bring a shaving kit.

Emergency Numbers
For police dial 100, fire service 101 and ambulance service 102. For medical requirements, the best hospital in town is the Apollo on Mathura Road, tel: 2692 5900.

---

there have been isolated cases of rape.

Try not to carry anything of value that you don't need – keep as much as you can, including travel documents and passports, locked up in the hotel safe. If you are unlucky enough to have something stolen, bear in mind that you'll have to report the theft to the police within 24 hours in order to be able to make an insurance claim.

Customs and Visas

Nationals of all countries except Nepal and Bhutan require a visa to enter India, however visitors from Finland, Japan, New Zealand, Singapore, Cambodia, Laos, Vietnam and the Philippines can now obtain a visa on arrival. Standard multiple-entry tourist visas are valid

for six months, and are available from any Indian Embassy, High Commission or Consulate worldwide. A new ruling means that anyone leaving India on a tourist visa cannot re-enter the country until a minimum of two months later.

Indian Customs allows nationals other than those from neighbouring states to bring 200 cigarettes, 50 cigars or 250 g of tobacco into India, as well as 1 litre of wine or spirits. Visitors can bring as much currency into the country as they like, but are not permitted to take any rupees out of the country without government clearance.

Electricity

Power supply is 220V 50Hz AC, via two- or three-pin round plugs. Supply can be erratic, particularly during the summer months, when air-conditioning units crank into life, massively increasing demand and leading to what is euphemistically referred to as 'load shedding' (power cuts). Supply is generally more stable at night.

Left: smoking a *huqqa* in Old Delhi.

Health

If you are careful there is no reason why you should be ill during your stay in Delhi. There are no vaccinations that are legally required to enter the country, but there are several that your doctor is likely to recommend strongly, including cholera, typhoid, hepatitis and tetanus. Outside of the monsoon season there is little need for malaria prophylaxis in Delhi, but do check on the current state of play with a nurse or pharmacist before you travel.

Keeping hydrated is important, but do not drink the tap water; try to stick to filtered and boiled water. For the same reason treat ice with suspicion, although you should be fine in upmarket bars and restaurants. Bottled water is available everywhere, but the environmental and social costs are extremely high, so it is best avoided. Fruit and salads are a possible source of infection. Only eat salads where you are sure they have been prepared in hygienic conditions, and stick to peeled fruit. Apply mosquito repellent and cover up in the evenings when you are most likely to be bitten.

DIARRHOEA

The most common problem encountered by overseas visitors is low-level food poisoning. Should you get stomach cramps, diarrhoea and vomiting, rest and drink plenty of fluids, including rehydration salts, available from most pharmacies; Electrol is the most common brand. Should the symptoms persist, or if you develop a fever or start passing blood or mucus, seek medical help. This is

best arranged through your hotel; if all else fails, the best hospital in town is the Apollo, on Mathura Road (tel: 2692 5858; www.apollohospdelhi.com). Travel insurance is essential, as the cost of treatment can be prohibitive.

Maps

The best map of Delhi is the Eicher map, which is available in two formats: a foldable paper form, good for general route-finding, or a much more detailed book, with every street name and locality listed. Locals tend to navigate by landmarks rather than street names, which they may not know at all. Hospitals and cinemas are the most popular terms of reference. A useful free map of Delhi is available from the tourist information desk in the arrivals hall of the international airport.

Media

The quality of the print media in India is generally good. Among the most popular papers are the *Times of India* and *Hindustan Times*, although the *Asian Age*, *The Hindu* and the *Indian Express* are considered to be more highbrow. There are also excellent weekly news magazines including *Outlook*, *India Today*, *Tehelka* and *Frontline*.

Most hotels will have satellite news TV channels such as NDTV, Times Now, BBC World and CNN.

Money

The rupee is theoretically divided into 100 paise; 0.5, 1, 2 and 5 rupee coins are available, as well as 2 (rare), 5, 10, 20, 50, 100, 500 and 1,000 rupee notes. Change is a perennial problem, as is finding anyone ready to admit they've actually got any. Be

---

From October 2008 the central government banned all smoking in public spaces, including bars and restaurants, reinforcing a similar ban (little enforced) that had been put in place by the state government in Delhi as long ago as 1997. This time the law has been far more strictly enforced.

---

desire for anonymity, websites are a key medium for young gay Indians to meet each other. Organisations such as **Sangama** (www.sangama.org) and **Sangini** (www.sanginii.org) campaign for gay and lesbian rights at a national and constitutional level, raise issues surrounding HIV infection (rates of which run very high in India) and offer support to the gay community.

The only long-standing gay male venue in Delhi is **Pegs and Pints** (Chanakya Lane, behind Akbar Bhavan, Chanakyapuri; tel: 2687 8320) on a Tuesday night. It is usually very crowded by 11pm but closes by 1am. It has a very friendly atmosphere (it is also popular with straight women wanting a fun night out). The cover charge is Rs 1,000.

particularly conscious of this when changing money and insist on having small denominations. In 2011, there were 45 rupees to US$1.

Travellers' cheques are safe but inconvenient, as changing them takes an awfully long time. It is better to rely on the extensive network of ATMs across the city (most will accept international cards – such as Maestro or Visa – and you will never be very far from one). Credit cards have become a common method of payment in Delhi, with most of the major international brands accepted.

Post

The Main GPO is at the intersection of Baba Khark Singh Marg and Ashok Road (Mon–Sat 10am–1pm, Sun 10am–1pm). This is the place where poste restante mail will be sent. For all other services, the post office in A Block, Connaught Place, is likely to be more convenient.

Postage rates are very reasonable, particularly for books, for which a separate rate applies. Parcels will need to be wrapped in cotton, stitched and sealed with wax, a process performed by the lines of specialists outside the post office. Consider using the 'Speed Post' service if your delivery is in any way urgent.

Telephone

The area code for Delhi is 011, and the country code for India 91. Numbers change with remarkable regularity, although all those here were correct at the time of going to press. Public phone booths are generally yellow and marked 'STD' (Standard Trunk Dialling) to denote national calls, and 'ISD' (International Subscriber Dialling) for international. Found dotted all over the city, these are manned operations; a machine calculates the cost of the call as soon as you hang up. Rates are low.

Even better are the rates on an Indian mobile phone. To get an Indian SIM card (Airtel have good rates and coverage) and number, foreign visitors must fill out a form and attach photographs and photocopy of their passport and visa. This is easily done, and many shops will perform this service for you; one good place is **Arihant Communications** (18 Main Market, Lodi Colony; tel: 2464 5303). Otherwise head for Ghaffar Market in Karol Bagh, where there are numerous places which will perform the same service.

Time Zone

Indian Standard Time is 5½ hours ahead of GMT. Daylight saving time is not observed.

Toilets

The Public Works Department in charge of public toilets, Sulabh, has some surprisingly well-maintained facilities in certain parts of the city. Users will be charged a Rs 2 entrance fee, and the toilets will generally be of the Indian, squatting design.

Tourist Information

Delhi's most helpful tourist office is the one run by India Tourism Delhi at 88 Janpath (tel: 2332 0342; www.incredible india.org). There is another branch at the aiport.

Websites

The **Archaeological Survey of India**:
www.asi.nic.in
The **Delhi Government** site:
www.delhigovt.nic.in
Delhi Tourism's official site:
www.delhitourism.nic.in
Clubbing and drinking:
www.explocity.com
Shopping and eating:
www.trendy.in
What's on when and where:
www.delhievents.com

Right: internet access is available all over Delhi.

41

Fashion

With its long-standing tradition of high-class textile production, exquisite embroidery and fine tailoring, it is not surprising that India has one of the most exciting fashion scenes in the world. The clothes on offer range from traditional *saris* and *salwar kamiz*, via beautifully cut Western-inspired work wear, to kooky and off-the-wall high-end fashion. With Indian designers starting to make a name for themselves on the international scene, Delhi is becoming one of the centres of world fashion, and has the boutiques and shops to prove it. Make sure you pack your credit card, 'cause some of it ain't cheap.

Where to Look

For those on a fashion mission the areas to explore are pretty much the same as for any other shopping trip. Some places, however, are special. The colony markets are obvious places to look, such as **Khan Market** and N and M Blocks in **Greater Kailash**, and the **Santushti Complex** is also worth a visit. **Lodi Colony Market** is currently designer central, with some of the biggest names in Indian fashion having their stores there. Of the shopping malls, **Select Citywalk Mall** in Saket, and Ambience Mall in Vasant Kunj, South Delhi, are good hunting grounds, particularly for western styles (although the prices are also western) but the most upmarket, fashion-dominated of them all is the **Crescent at the Qutab** in Lado Sarai (opposite the Qutb Minar Complex). For more traditional clothes, but with a designer twist, the boutiques of **Hauz Khas Village** are worth browsing through.

SEE ALSO SHOPPING, P.120

Above: comfy clothes piled high at Fabindia.

Connaught Place

People Tree

8 Regal Building, Sansad Marg; tel: 2334 0699; www.people treeonline.com; Mon–Sat 10.30am–7pm; metro: Rajiv Chowk; map p.137 C4

Unusual ethnic-style clothing, jewellery, stationery and wacky T-shirts are the hallmark of this organic little operation, often made exclusively for their own brand label. Note that this People Tree has nothing to do with the UK-based clothing company of the same name.

Rajpath and Chanakyapuri

Ensemble

36 Santushti Shopping Complex, Chanakyapuri; tel: 2688 2207; www.ensembleindia.com; Mon–Sat 10am–6pm; metro: Race Course; map p.136 B2

Set up by Indian fashion superstar Tarun Tahiliani over 20 years ago, Ensemble is still one of the best places to find clothes by cutting-edge and top-flight Indian fashion designers. Almost painfully chic, with plenty to drool over, Ensemble is a must-visit.

Left: designer *salwar kamiz* on display in Hauz Khas.

not date but are still fashionable. Not content with restricting this to clothing, they have branched out into accessories and interior design.

Anokhi

32 Khan Market; tel: 2460 3423; www.anokhi.com; Mon–Sat 10am–8pm; metro: Khan Market; map p.137 D2

Anokhi's clothing is a favourite of visitors – both men and women – of a certain age who have been coming to India for years. The loose, comfortable designs made from high-quality cotton are cool in the sun and keep you covered up. Perhaps a little on the traditional side, but if that is what you are after then they don't come any better than this. Also in the Santushti Complex and N Block Market, Greater Kailash I.

Fabindia

Central Hall, above Shops 20–21, Khan Market; tel: 4368 3100;

Most top European fashion houses, such as Jean-Paul Gaultier, Dior, Balenciaga and Armani, have their embroidery and appliqué work done in India. Some of this is done by Indian fashion houses, such as that of the Mumbai based-designer Gayatri Khanna, but also by specialist fabric producers. To find some of these exquisite Indian fabrics have a look around the fabric bazaar of Katra Neel in Old Delhi.

Ogaan

4A Santushti Shopping Complex, Chanakyapuri; tel: 2467 2429; www.kavitabhartia.com; Mon–Sat 10am–6pm; metro: Race Course; map p.136 B2

Set up by designer Kavita Bhartia, Ogaan sells a selection from the latest collections of top Indian names such as Ashish Soni and J.J. Valaya, as well as up-and-coming young designers. The store at Santushti is more geared towards a Western look, with the outlets at Khan Market and Hauz Khas tending more towards an Indian aesthetic.

Padakkam

17 Santushti Shopping Complex, Chanakyapuri; tel: 2467 1417; www. padakkam.net; Mon–Sat 10am–6pm; metro: Race Course; map p.136 B2

Padakkam has exquisite *saris* and *salwar kamiz* mostly from South India, all in the most beautiful fabrics. As well as some accessories, they have also branched out into classy Western separates. They also have two outlets in Gurgaon.

Lodi Gardens and Nizamuddin

Abraham and Thakore

DLF Emporio Mall, Vasant Kunj; tel: 4606 0995; www.abraham andthakore.com; daily 11am–7.30pm; metro: Haus Khas then rickshaw; map p.137 D1

Very elegant and very chic, the clothes of David Abraham and Rakesh Thakore are perennial favourites in Delhi. Made of beautiful natural fabrics and with excellent cutting skills, both their mens- and womensware lines provide classics that will

Right: Ranna Gill in Khan Market, *see p.44.*

Above: Samsaara in South Extension II is a superb place to pick up clothes by a range of top Indian designers.

www.fabindia.com; daily 10am–8pm; metro: Khan Market; map p.137 D2

Fabindia designs are well cut and flattering, and the tops in particular would not look out of place anywhere. The quality of the fabrics and the sewing is very high. There are also branches at, among other places: B28 Connaught Place; 5, 7 and 14 N Block Market, Greater Kailash I; Karol Bagh, Lajpat Nagar and Vasant Kunj.

Manish Arora
3 Main Market, Lodi Colony; tel: 2463 8878; www.manish arora.ws; daily 11am–7.30pm; metro: Jor Bagh; map p.137 D1

Vivid and vibrant, Manish Arora's clothes are boggling in their use of bold colours, off-the-wall ideas and exuberant appliqué – designs for which the term funky doesn't go halfway to describing. Current looks include pseudo-gladiator armour with a dash of Venetian carnival. Also at G10, Crescent at the Qutab, Lado Sarai,

For information on Indian designers, see the website of the **Fashion Design Council of India** (www.fdci.org), which has links to many of the designers' own websites. Another good source is **Vogue India** (www.vogue.in), which has lots of fashion news and shoots of the latest collections.

South Delhi.

Rajesh Pratap Singh
9 Lodi Colony Market; tel: 3262 4722; www.pratap.ws; daily 11am–7.30pm; metro: Jor Bagh; map p.137 D1

The maker of some of the best menswear to be found in Delhi, as well as fresh and elegant womenswear. Originally from Rajasthan, Rajesh Pratap Singh has brought all the traditional tailoring skills of his home state to bear on his creations, and the result is some of the best-cut clothes to be had in the capital.

Ranna Gill
53A Khan Market; tel: 4175 7700; www.rannagill.com; daily 10am–7pm; metro: Khan Market; map p.137 D2

Drawing on her training in India and New York, Ranna Gill produces beautifully draped dresses, with many of her pieces having elegant, classical lines. These are combined with interesting prints to give a distinctive look to her clothes. Also at F12 The Crescent at the Qutab and 41 Santushti Shopping Complex.

Satya Paul
B105 Defence Colony; tel: 5155 2568; www.satyapaul.com; daily 10.30am–7pm; metro: Lajpat Nagar; map p.139 D4

One of the country's most established designers, who has retained his quirky eye for all things Indian. His stores have something for

Right: shoes in South Extension II; handbags in Khan Market.

everyone, from neat and colourful skirts and tops to sumptuous *saris* and fashionable *salwar kamiz*. As well as this outlet, he can be found at The Crescent at the Qutb and M55 Greater Kailash I.

Tarun Tahiliani Boutique
D19 Defence Colony; tel: 4155 3237; www.taruntahiliani.com; daily 10.30am–7pm; metro: Lajpat Nagar; map p.139 D4

As well as being featured at Ensemble, this is the named boutique for Tahiliani. His signature fusion of Indian and Western produces some elegant clothes; a good place to head for if you need something for a special occasion.

South Delhi

Cottons
N11, Greater Kailash I; tel: 4163 5108; daily 10am–7pm. metro: East of Kailash; map p.139 D3

Classic hand-printed cotton wear, mostly for ladies but with a small gents' section as well. Slightly less predictable than Fabindia and Anokhi, but along the same general lines.

Magnetic Rag
Archana Arcade, Greater Kailash I; tel: 4163 4970; www.gauriand

nainika.com; daily 10.30am–7pm; metro: East of Kailash; map p.139 E2

The young pair of designers Gauri and Nainika Karan are ones to watch. They have made a great impact with their recent collections of Western dresses and separates. Young, trendy and feminine are three words often used to describe their clothes. Their work is also available at Ogaan in the Santushti Shopping Complex.

Samsaara
E21 South Extension Market II; tel: 4323 9000; www.samsaara. in; daily 10.30am–8.30pm; metro: INA; map p.139 E2

Set up by the holding company of designers such as Satya Paul, Samsaara was created as a one-stop shop for top-end Indian designers. The beautifully laid-out store contains clothes by, among others, Rohit Bal, Manish Malhotra, J.J Valaya and Satya Paul, and ranges from traditional wedding wear to classic separates and sexy dresses, in addition to a good range of menswear.

Mehrauli and Tughlaqabad

Ritu Kumar
F12 The Crescent at the Qutab, Lado Sarai; tel: 3291 2542; www.ritukumar.com; daily 11am–7.30pm; metro: Qutab Minar; map p.138 B1

One of India's most successful designers, Ritu Kumar has three lines that sell in a chain of shops across the country with high-quality but still relatively affordable clothes that retain a strong link with Indian traditions. She also has a line in trendy accessories.

Rohit Bal
218–219, 2nd Floor, C2 District Centre, Saket; tel: 2956 2895; www.rohitbal.com; daily 10am–7pm; metro: Saket; map p.138 B1

One of India's most impressive designers and one with an international profile. Rohit Bal's clothes are often sculptural and set out to make an impression. Think high collars, crisp tailoring and puffball skirts, to name some of his recent preoccupations. His *prêt-à-porter* diffusion line, Balance, can be found at The Crescent at the Qutab.

Festivals and Events

In a country almost suffering from a surfeit of religion – being home to, among others, Hindus, Muslims, Buddhists, Sikhs, Jains and Christians – it is inevitable that there will be a large number of religious festivals spread throughout the year. Not all of these are official public holidays (see the box below for those that are), but you may find that in particular areas shops and businesses close during certain festivals. As well as the religious festivals there are numerous secular ones devoted to politics, culture and other events.

January

Lohri

This festival celebrates the peak of winter, marked by bonfires, singing and dancing.

Republic Day

26 January, the date the constitution of Independent India came into force, is marked by a parade of military might (the decorated camels of the Border Security Force are a popular spectacle), folk dancing and colourful floats.

February–March

Surajkund Crafts Mela

A huge crafts fair is held at Surajkund, 5km (3 miles) south of Tughlaqabad.

Garden Festival

Delhi Tourism organises this festival of gardening at the Garden of the Five Senses in Mehrauli.

Jahan-e-Khusrau

This three-day Sufi music festival, celebrating the great musician Amir Khusrau, takes place in the grounds of Humayun's Tomb.

The Statesman Vintage Car Rally

This annual event has been going since 1964. A proces-

Public holidays with fixed dates are:

26 January **Republic Day**

15 March **Holi**

1 May **Labour Day**

15 August **Independence Day**

5 November **Guru Nanak's Birthday**

25 December **Christmas Day**

Precise dates of religious festivals are calculated according to astrological and lunar calendars, and are therefore subject to change. Public holidays with movable dates are:

January **Bakr Id**

February **Muharram**

March/April **Good Friday**

April **Navami Id Milad**

May **Buddha Purnima**

October **Dussehra**

November **Divali**

---

sion of vintage and classic cars is flagged off from Statesman House on Barakhamba Road. Prizes are given out to the best-maintained cars.

Holi

This North Indian festival marks the end of winter and the onset of spring, and is celebrated by throwing

---

coloured paint mixed with water at friends, neighbours and passers-by. Traditionally this is a time of *mast*, intoxication, and some people drink *bhang lassi* (*lassi* laced with cannabis). Women should be very careful if they venture out on their own, and no one should wear their best clothes.

Mahasivaratri

This celebrates the god Siva's dance of preservation to save the world.

April

Vaisakhi

This is the Sikh New Year, and also celebrates the founding of the *Khalsa*, the Sikh brotherhood.

August–September

Independence Day

15 August is marked by particularly animated celebrations at the Lal Qila, where a flag is ritually raised to signify India's independence from British rule. The prime minister gives a speech (effectively India's 'state of the union' address) from the top of the Lahore Gate.

Left: the Urs of Nizamuddin is celebrated with music.

December

Christmas and New Year
These are celebrated mostly in Christian households, but with less fuss than in the West.

Moveable Festivals

Ramadan
The Muslim month of fasting, moves back by about 11 days each year.

Id-ul-Fitr
This marks the end of Ramadan, and is particularly heartily celebrated in Old Delhi.

Urs of Nizamuddin
About two weeks after Id, this celebrates the anniversary of the saint's death.

Muharram
In Old Delhi Shi'a Muslims celebrate the death of Hussain, grandson of the Prophet, with processions carrying *tazias*, large constructions that represent his tomb at Karbala.

Bakr Id
The 'feast of the sacrfice' commemorates Ibrahim's willingness to sacrifce his son. It takes place at the time of the *Haj* to Makkah.

Janmashtami
Krishna's birthday is traditionally celebrated by the performance of *Ras lilas*, plays that enact events from his life.
SEE ALSO LITERATURE AND THEATRE, P.73

October

Phulwalon-Ki-Sair
The 'Flower Sellers' Procession' centres around the Qutb Minar, and involves processions of large fans of flowers aimed at promoting communal harmony; it is celebrated by both Hindus and Muslims.

Navaratri
This is the nine-day festival of the goddess Durga; it culminates in Dussehra *(see below)*. During this period the *Ram lila* is performed (the *Ram lila* ground is near New Delhi station).
SEE ALSO LITERATURE AND THEATRE, P.73

Dussehra
This festival celebrates both the goddess Durga's victory over Mahisasura (the buffalo demon) and Rama's triumph over the demon Ravana, of whom huge effigies are made and then ritually burnt on the last of the 10 days of the festival; often packed with fireworks, the effigies literally go up with a bang.

The Qutb Festival
This takes place nightly at the **Qutb Minar Complex**, starting at 6.30pm, and features performances by some of the best national and international singers of Sufi music, as well as performances of Hindustani and Karnatak music and classical dance.
SEE ALSO MONUMENTS, P.82

October–November

Delhi Half Marathon
This normally takes place in November, when the heat is slightly less gruelling.
SEE ALSO SPORT, P.125

Divali (Dipavali)
The festival of lights and fireworks celebrates Rama and Sita's homecoming after their exile in the *Ramayana*. Festivities include illuminating houses by the lighting of oil lamps and firecrackers, and the exchanging of sweets and gifts.

Guru Purab
On this day the Sikhs celebrate the birth of Guru Nanak.

Much to the disgust of hard-line Hindu fanatics, recent years have seen the Western festivals of Valentine's Day and Halloween adopted with increasing enthusiasm by, largely, middle-class India. Never ones to let up on some kitsch, just before 14 February card shops, such as the popular chain Archies, are flooded with soppy greetings cards and florists see a rise in business, while with the approach of 31 October supermarkets suddenly acquire a range of gruesome masks and faux pumpkins.

Film

Think of entertainment in India and you are bound to imagine the cinema. The biggest film industry in the world is characterised by big blockbusters that incorporate love stories, action and violence, song-and-dance routines and often gaudy sets and set pieces that inhabit an imaginary world of glamour with an at times eye-wateringly tasteless array of costumes and consumption. The people of Delhi are as addicted to these Bollywood blockbusters as any other North Indians, and taking in a movie while you are in the city is an essential part of the whole experience.

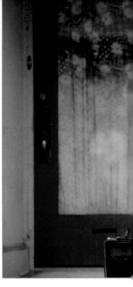

Glamour and Money

While the popular perception is that Bollywood cinema is all shaking hips and wet *saris* – and there is some truth in this characterisation – the films are perhaps best seen as morality plays – good versus evil plays a prominent part, drawing on some of the conventions of traditional Indian theatre. Also, in recent years, more nuanced films have explored traditionally grey areas of morality (such as affairs and divorce in *Kabhi Alvida Naa Kehna*) or idealistic notions of unity and difference (in films from *Amar, Akbar, Anthony* to *Chak De India*). Huge amounts of money are made and invested in the cinema, and there have long been accusations of Bollywood's connections with the Mumbai underworld, perhaps adding an extra frisson of glamour for its vast number of adoring fans.

The Birth of Bollywood

In Hindi the mainstream blockbusters are made in Mumbai – known as Bolly-

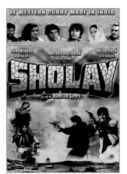

Above: poster for the hugely influential *Sholay*.

wood from a combination of 'Bombay' and 'Hollywood' – often cited as having the largest film industry in the world. It is, however, run a close second by the South Indian industry (that has, at times, outstripped its northern rival). South India has even given Bollywood some of its biggest stars; Sri Devi, Aishwarya Rai and A.R. Rahman have all made the transition to Hindi movies.

The first, silent, film made in India was *Raja Harishchandra* (1913), filmed in Mumbai.

While the early 'silents' were popular and the industry grew considerably during the 1920s, it was not until the advent of the 'talkies' in 1931 that India's close and passionate affair with the movies began in earnest. These early films were quite racy, featuring plenty of flesh and kissing, and it was not until Independence in 1947 that a form of 'moral censorship' came into play. The banning of the on-screen kiss and physical contact between a film's lovers led to inventive ways around the problem, and a whole host of wet-*sari* scenes, suggestive dances around trees and just-in-time fades.

Until the 1970s most films were romances, and the on-screen loves of stars such as Nargis and Sunil Dutt (who became real-life lovers after starring in *Mother India*, 1957) and Madhubala and Raj Kapoor were all consuming topics of discussion among their many fans. This changed in the 1970s with the arrival of a new generation of actors, includ-

Left: Rizwan Khan in the blockbuster *My Name is Khan*.

ing Amitabh Bachchan. His appearance in the 1975 mega-hit *Sholay* ushered in an era of action movies, dubbed 'Curry Westerns' in homage to the Italian movies that inspired them.

While *Sholay* played on an appetite for violence, the 1990s saw the rebirth of the family drama and romance. Films such as *Hum Aapke Hain Hum*, *Raja Hindustani* and *Maine Pyar Kiya* managed the difficult task of promoting traditional family values while chaste but scantily clad actresses and muscle-bound heroes flirt and revel in material excess. In Bollywood these included Karisma Kapoor and Madhuri Dixit as well as Salman and Amir Khan.

Recent Films

While more 'art house' films from India have achieved audiences outside of the Subcontinent – such as Meera Nair's *Monsoon Wedding* (2001) and Deepa

Right: scene from the hit comedy *3 Idiots*.

The most comfortable places to catch up with the latest releases (in Hindi and English) are the **PVR multiplexes** (cinemas and listings can be found at www.pvrcinemas.com) located all over Delhi and Gurgaon. The most attractive venue, however, is the restored **Plaza Cinema** on Connaught Place, first opened in 1933.

Mehta's *Fire* (1996) – Bollywood has now gained a following outside of South Asian communities. This has been helped in part through

the prevalence of bland, location-neutral (or US- or Europe-based) films. The biggest-grossing Indian film ever outside of South Asia was *3 Idiots* (2009); the biggest-grossing film in India, however, was *My Name is Khan*, released in 2010, which earned three times as much.

Recently Bollywood actors and actresses have found other ways to gain fame abroad; Shilpa Shetty's headline-grabbing encounter with the UK's *Big Brother* in 2007 raised the profile of the industry (even if she subsequently found herself in trouble back home after being kissed in public by Richard Gere).

The trade goes both ways, however, with the 'Big B' (as Amitabh Bachchan is known) revitalising his career through hosting *Kaun Banega Crorepati* (India's *Who Wants to be a Millionaire?*). However, his successor on the show, (Shah Rukh Khan), has recently found his television career in the doldrums after the collapse of the much-trailed *Kya aap Panchvi Pass Se Tez Hain?*

49

Food and Drink

Eating in Delhi can be a real treat. From the exquisite Mughal dishes found in some of the top hotel restaurants to the street food of Old Delhi, it is generally tasty and not a little spicy (the chilli heat can be usefully deflected by eating or drinking yoghurt in the form of a *raita* or *lassi*). Those who are used to 'Indian' food back home may be in for a shock, as the dishes on offer generally bear little relation to those found in restaurants in Europe or North America. Many Indians are vegetarian, and visiting herbivores will have little trouble finding good things to eat. *See also Restaurants, p.112–19.*

Punjabi and Mughlai

While the quality of Delhi's Indian-cuisine restaurants and food stalls has never been in doubt, recent years have seen a significant hike in the quality and variety of international offerings, making Delhi a real eating destination at last. The Punjabi influence has permeated much of Delhi's daily life, and the food is no exception. The same dish is never the same twice, and in some cases can be entirely different from one restaurant, or *dhaba*, to another.

Vegetarian dishes tend to revolve around *dal* (lentils) in either black or yellow guise, *panir* (often translated as cottage cheese, it has a similarly neutral taste but is more tofu-like in texture) and green vegetables including spinach, peas, okra, peppers and cauliflower. Chicken, and 'butter chicken' in particular, his the standard 'non-veg' offering, with mutton often an option as well.

Mughlai cuisine is quite similar to Punjabi but ostensibly more sophisticated, the

Above: green chillies and slices of white radish on a *thali*, a common relish.

> Although typically heavy on butter and *ghi* (clarified butter), good Punjabi dishes are uniquely filling yet full of surprisingly delicate and varied tastes.

recipes having been handed down from the kitchens of the Mughal emperors. While the very best exponents of the Mughlai school produce a variety and combination of different tastes and textures that are nothing short of

exquisite, there are a number of Punjabi restaurants aimed at tourists which have simply re-branded their standard fare as Mughlai in a bid to justify inflated prices.

South Indian and Snacks

South Indian cuisine is increasingly well represented in Delhi, and *masala dosa*, an outsized savoury pancake made from fermented rice-flour batter rolled into a tube and filled with a combination of

Left: grilled *panir* at Karim's, Old Delhi.

pretty much the norm. The reality, however, is that all the dishes served in this type of 'multi-cuisine' restaurant will generally have something of India in them (so-called 'Chinjabi' food), with both the Chinese and Continental offerings likely to be liberally laced with Indian spices. Dishes such as pasta or even salads are often dismissed as 'bland' unless enlivened with liberal amounts of chilli powder.

There are, however, a number of exceptional Chinese eateries, generally distinguishable by the lack of Indian dishes on their menus, as well as some excellent Italian, Lebanese and 'fusion' restaurants. Happily for the wallets of the upmarket Delhi diner, these places are no longer found solely in the city's five-star hotels, a development which has much improved the dining scene.

Rotis and Thalis

Favourites for breakfast include *puri* and *paratha*, a fried, flat bread most commonly stuffed with potato

potato, onions, coconut, chilli and mustard seeds, is a favourite; an absolute treat when you come across a good one. There are also a couple of decent South Indian chains with a wider range on offer. Mumbai's street snack, *chaat*, is also easily found as are popular staples such as *pao bhaji* (a red-lentil-and-tomato-based sauce accompanied by a white bread roll) and *bhel puri* (puffed rice, vermicelli, potato and puri-style bread mixed with onions, tomatoes, coriander and lemon juice), available from stalls all over the city.

Seafood can be hard to get hold of; traditional wisdom dictates that in a place this far from the sea, and without reliable refrigerated transport, the freshness of seafood in the summer months must be open to question. Having said that, there are a number of specialist restaurants which fly

their produce in daily, and are well worth trying.

Chinjabi and Chilli

The number-one non-Indian cuisine is without doubt Chinese. A word of warning: Indian restaurants tend to be very ambitious in the range and scope of the dishes that they offer. Indeed, few mid-range places offer just one type of cuisine; a menu with a vast array of Indian, Chinese and Continental dishes is

Right: a crowded stall in the Khari Baoli spice market, Old Delhi, *see p.53.*

It seems that one of Delhi's culinary glories, its street food, could soon disappear. In 2007 the Supreme Court upheld a city-authority ban on cooking in the open air that would force the more than 300,000 stalls to close. There has been considerable discontent over the idea and so far the ban has had little effect, so in the meantime head for places like Chandni Chowk to gorge yourself on delicious *chana* (chickpeas), *puri* and *paratha* (fried breads) and *samosa*. Make sure you choose your stall carefully though: one of the reasons the authorities wish to close them down is they claim many of the stalls are unhygienic.

and green chillies and served with some sort of 'chutney'. These are not chutneys as known in the West, but instead fiery concoctions aimed at adding zest to a meal, to be consumed in small quantities. There's a massive array of options for eating in the middle of the day, although the Punjabi-style dishes can be slightly heavy for a midday meal. A

thali, a large metal dish with a combination of rice and bread in its centre, surrounded by up to 10 small metal bowls containing a wide variety of both sweet and savoury dishes, can make an excellent alternative. Not only very good value, they're also a great way of tasting a lot of dishes at the same time, and working out which ones you particularly like. They are found at both North and South Indian restaurants, and often change on a daily basis.

Drinks

Chai (sweet, milky tea) is served everywhere, and is safe to drink. It generally comes in 'ready-made' form everywhere, meaning that cut tea leaves (or more often tea 'dust') are boiled together with milk and sugar to produce an invigorating and much-loved beverage. Coffee served on the street tends to be remarkably similar.

Lassi, a yoghurt-based drink often served after a meal, or as a refreshing snack at other times, can take some getting used to,

but is invaluable for its cooling properties, particularly after a spicy meal. It comes in all sorts of flavours: plain, sweet or salty are the basic options, but specialist *lassi-wallas* will have a whole range on offer.

Local beers (such as the ubiquitous Kingfisher) and spirits (known as 'Indian Made Foreign Liquor' or IMFL) are widely available, with wine starting to gain popularity. Indian producers are now making wine which is, if not world-class, certainly very drinkable and significantly cheaper than imported wine, which tends to be available only in the five-star hotels. The three labels to look out for are Sula, Grover and Marquise de Pompadour.

Delhi Specials

Ghantewala

1862A Chandni Chowk, Old Delhi; tel: 2328 0490; Mon–Sat 8am–9pm; metro: Chandni Chowk; map p.135 D3

This, the most famous sweet shop in Old Delhi (where

Right: boxed or loose at the Mittal Tea House.

Left: Old Delhi's street food is delicious.

there is some competition), has been here for years. Its deliciously sticky *barfi*, *jalebis* and *halva* are worth a trip all on their own.

Khari Baoli

Chandni Chowk, Old Delhi; Mon–Sat 11am–8pm; metro: Chandni Chowk; map p.135 C3

This huge spice market is the place to come to find ingredients; if you can't find it here then there is a good chance it doesn't exist.

Mittal Tea House

8A Main Market, Lodi Colony; tel: 2461 5709; Mon–Sat 10am–8pm; metro: Jor Bagh; map p.137 D1

This shop has a staggering number of fine teas, from Assam and Darjeeling in India to rare offerings from China and Japan.

Food Vocabulary (Hindi)

I want (a thali) *Mujhe (thali) chahiye*
Without chilli *Mirch ke bina*
Little chilli *Kam mirch*
Hot *Garam*
Cold *Thanda*
Ripe/cooked *Pukka*

BASICS

Biriyani Rice cooked with vegetables or meat
Chaval Rice
Dahi Yoghurt
Dudh Milk
Ghi Clarified butter
Kofta Dumpling or ball
Lassi Yoghurt drink
Makhan Butter
Malai Cream
Masala Mix or marinade of spices
Mirch Chilli
Namak Salt
Nimbu pani Lime water
Pani Water
Paneer Cheese
Pilao Rice cooked with *ghi* and spices
Raita Yoghurt with cucumber
Samosa Deep-fried parcel of meat or vegetables
Tandoor Oven

BREADS (ROTI)

Chapatti Flat, unleavened bread
Nan Leavened flat bread
Pappad Fried, crisp bread made from ground lentils
Paratha *Chapatti* cooked with *ghi*
Puri Deep-fried and puffed-up wheat bread
Tandoori roti Similar to *nan*

VEGETABLES (SUBZI)

Aloo Potato
Baigan/brinjal Aubergine
Bindi Okra
Chana Chickpeas
Dal Dried pulses
Gobi Cauliflower
Kumbh Mushroom
Mutter Peas
Palak/Sag Spinach
Pyaz Onion
Rajma Red kidney beans
Sarsun Mustard greens
Tamata Tomato

MEAT

Gosht Lamb
Machli Fish
Murg Chicken

SWEETS (MITHAI)

Gulab jamun Deep-fried dough balls soaked in syrup
Halva A sweetmeat of vegetables, fruit, nuts and sugar
Jalebi Spirals of deep-fried, syrup-soaked batter
Kheer A milk-based pudding
Kulfi A milk-based frozen pudding

FRUIT

Aum Mango
Kela Banana
Santara Orange

SEE ALSO LANGUAGE, P.68–9

Forts

Delhi is dotted with the remains of the fortifications thrown up by successive waves of invaders. These forts tell the history of the city, and are identified as the different 'cities' of Delhi, from the early forts of the Rajputs and massive ramparts of Tughlaqabad in the south, via Firoz Shah Kotla and the early-Mughal Purana Qila, to the Unesco World Heritage Site of the Lal Qila of Old Delhi, Shah Jahan's palace-fort and a symbol of the city. Searching out some of these places can feel quite adventurous and will take you off the beaten track into parts of Delhi not often explored by visitors.

Above: keeping the Lal Qila neat and tidy.

Old Delhi and Raj Ghat

Firoz Shah Kotla

Bahadur Shah Zafar Marg; daily sunrise–sunset; entrance charge; metro: Pragati Maidan; map p.135 E1

Built by Firoz Shah Tughlaq (1351–88), this citadel once lay on the banks of the Yamuna. Little now remains of the splendour of Firoz Shah's capital, as much of the useful stone was carted off in the 17th century to build what is now Old Delhi.

The fort was made up of two large quadrangles. The northern ruins are set in a pleasant park which you enter through a large barbicaned gate. Inside, the most remarkable monument resembles a pyramid, on top of which stands a polished stone Ashokan pillar. Also here are a *baoli* (step well) and the ruined remains of Firoz Shah's Jama Masjid. Both the *baoli* and Jama Masjid ruins have underground rooms that can still be explored.

Lal Qila

Lal Qila, Old Delhi; www.asi. nic.in; Tue–Sun sunrise–sunset; entrance charge; metro: Chandni Chowk; map p.135 D3

The spectacular Lal Qila (Red Fort, so called because of the colour of its sandstone walls) faces Chandni Chowk (meaning 'moonlit' or 'silver crossroads'), once the central avenue of a bazaar that is still an important commercial centre. Listed as a Unesco World Heritage Site in 2007, it is the most

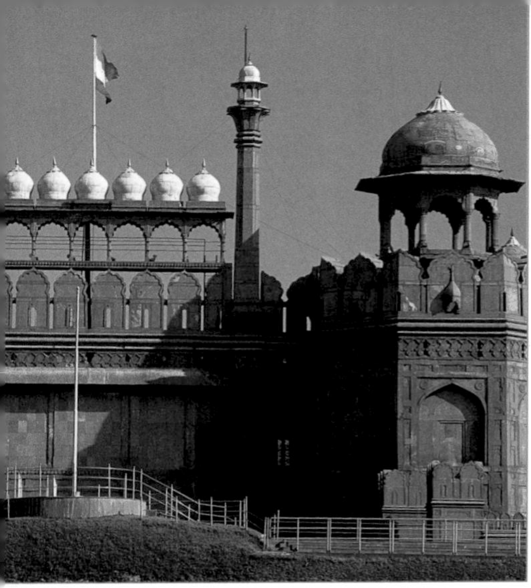

Left: the Lahore Gate of the Lal Qila.

Although it may be a little hard to visualise now, the Lal Qila was intended by Shah Jahan to be a pleasure palace as well as an impregnable fortification. To aid in this, the fort was laid out with beautiful gardens through which ran rivulets of water from the Nahr-i-Bihisht, the 'stream of paradise' that originated from a tank within the fort and then flowed out down neighbouring Chandni Chowk. The stream collected in a pool, which reflected the moonlight that shone along the street.

impressive Mughal monument in the city. Shah Jahan, the Mughal emperor whose paradise this was, began the building of the immense red sandstone fort with its palaces and halls in 1639, and it was completed nine years later.

The entry point is **Lahore Gate**. Inside, passing through the Chatta Chowk covered market, one enters Shah Jahan's elaborate gardens. To the far right is the **Mumtaz Mahal**, possibly a former harem and now the **Archaeological Museum** with a collection of Mughal artefacts including miniatures, porcelain and costumes.

Next to the museum are the Rang Mahal and Khas Mahal, the emperor's private apartments. The **Rang Mahal** is made of pure marble with a beautiful basin in the centre shaped like the petals of a lotus, which used to have a silver fountain on it.

The octagonal tower **Shah Burj** was used for royal public appearances (including that of Britain's George V and Queen Mary during their visit to India in 1931). The **Diwan-e-Am** (public audience hall) is particularly impressive, with a marble throne at its centre surrounded by *pietra dura* inlay. Other buildings include the royal baths and the tiny white marble **Moti Masjid** (Pearl Mosque).

A famous Persian couplet by Shah Jahan's court poet Amir Khusrau ('If there be paradise on the face of earth/ It is this! Oh it is this! Oh it is this!') is inscribed on the walls of the **Diwan-e-Khas** (private audience hall), giving some idea of how the interior of the fort must have appeared. The Diwan-e-Khas once housed the legendary Peacock Throne and the Koh-i-noor diamond, but these were looted when the Persian Nadir Shah sacked Delhi in 1739. Opposite is the **Naqqara Khana**, a sandstone ceremonial gateway, so called because the *naqqara khana* (ceremonial ensemble consisting of trumpets and kettledrums, *naqqara*) played from its balconies to mark the hours of the day or the arrival and departure of the emperor and his retinue.

Now that the Yamuna has retreated, the fort, originally built on its banks, overlooks a large open ground, previously the site of Chor Bazaar (the 'thieves' market', now held near the Jama Masjid).

SEE ALSO MUSEUMS AND GALLERIES, P.85

Salimgarh Fort
Mahatma Gandhi Marg, Salimgarh, Old Delhi; daily 10am–5pm; free; metro:

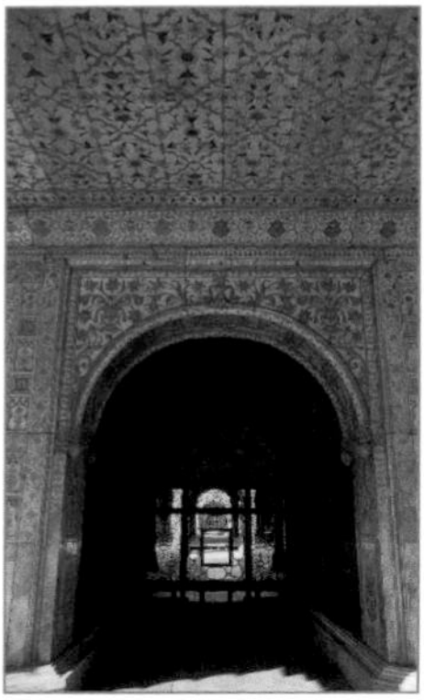

Right: exquisite decoration in the Lal Qila.

Chandni Chowk; map p.135 D3
This smaller fort lies just to the north of the Lal Qila. It was originally built by Salim Shah in 1546 on what was then an island in the Yamuna. As the river moved eastwards the defensive position became less valuable, but it was still used by Aurangzeb as a prison, and that tradition was carried on by the British, who used the fort to bang up members of the Indian National Army (INA: Indians who fought against the British during World War II in the hope that it would hasten independence for the country). Part of the fort now contains the **Swatantrata Senani Museum** dedicated to the INA.
SEE ALSO MUSEUMS AND GALLERIES, P.86

Rajpath and Chanakyapuri

Purana Qila
Off Mathura Road, beside Pragati Maidan; www.asi.nic.in; daily sunrise–sunset; entrance charge, includes entry into the Archaeological Museum; metro: Pragati Maidan; map p.137 E3
The Old Fort (from the Urdu *purana*, 'old', and *qila*, 'fort') was built by Afghan ruler Sher Shah Suri (1540–45) and was taken over by Mughal emperor

> Purana Qila is said to mark the spot of the legendary city of Indraprastha, capital of the Pandavas, heroes of the Hindu epic, *the Mahabarata*.

Humayun when he regained the throne in 1555–6. There was a village called Inderpat (derived from Indraprastha) actually inside the walls of the fort until the British moved it out at the time of the construction of New Delhi. During excavations here Painted Grey Ware was found, dating back to around 1000 BC, and pointing to a long history of human settlement.

Inside the beautifully maintained grounds is the **Qila-e-Kunha-Masjid**, the best-preserved Lodi mosque in Delhi. It was built by Sher Shah in 1541 on one of the highest points in the fort. The mosque is midway in style between the solid mosques of the Delhi Sultanate and the graceful ones of the later Mughal period.

Just to the right inside the main gate is the fort's **Archaeological Museum**, containing artefacts from the excavations on the site.

The **Sher Mandal** pavilion is a beautifully proportioned

pavilion in the middle of the well-maintained gardens. This is said to have been used as a library and was where the Mughal emperor Humayun fell to his death.

Outside the main entrance is an attractive park and lake (once part of the moat) surrounding the fort.
SEE ALSO MUSEUMS AND GALLERIES, P.87

South Delhi

Siri Fort
Off Khel Gaon Marg; daily sunrise–sunset; free; metro: Green Park; map p.139 D3
A few last remains of Siri's outer walls can be made out in the undergrowth. The fort was purpose-built to try to defend Emperor Ala-ud-din and his people from attacks by marauding Mongols, who were fond of invading Delhi and in 1298 managed to ransack the city's suburbs.

So unchallenged did they feel that a large number of Mongols chose to stay on in Delhi once the attack was over, a mistake they would live to regret. Having been forced to retreat as far back as the area around the Qutb

Right: the huge ramparts of the fort of Tughlaqabad.

Left: the ramparts and
the Sher Mandal in the
Purana Qila.

Minar, Ala-ud-din went on a
rampage of his own once the
coast was clear. Every
remaining Mongol in Delhi
was murdered, their severed
heads first put on public display and then incorporated
into the walls of Siri Fort, the
building of which had just
begun. Whereas most of
Delhi's cities were named
after their founder, Siri is
derived from the Hindi word
sir, meaning 'head'.

Mehrauli and
Tughlaqabad

Adilabad and Nai ka Kot
Off Mehrauli–Badarpur Road;
daily sunrise–sunset; free
metro: Tughlaqabad
These two small fortified sites
are close to Tughlaqabad.
Adilabad seems to have been
built by Muhammad bin
Tughlaq, while Nai ka Kot is
probably the first fort built by
Ghazi Malik.
Lal Kot and Qila
Rai Pithora
Off Kalkadas Marg, Mehrauli
Archaeological Park; daily

sunrise–sunset; free; metro:
Qutab Minar; map p.138 B1
The ruined walls of the
fortress of the Tomar Rajputs
(8th–12th century) can be
seen on the outskirts of
Mehrauli Village. These were
then incorporated into the
southern walls of Qila Rai
Pithora, the city of the later
Chauhan Rajputs who ruled
during the 12th century.
Tughlaqabad Fort
Off the Mehrauli–Badarpur Road;
daily sunrise– sunset; entrance
charge; metro: Tughlaqabad; map
p.139 E1
A few kilometres due south
of the Baha'i Lotus Temple
stand the massive walls of
Tughlaqabad, the third city
of Delhi, built by the first of
the Tughlaq rulers, Ghazi
Malik, in the 1320s. Houses,
palaces and temples once
stood here; today, it is the
city walls, 6 km (4 miles) in
circumference, that are most
prominent, and give the best
impression of the scale of
this vast city. As well as a
large, deep tank called the
jahannum ka rasta (the 'gateway to hell'), the most
prominent monument within
the fort is the **Vijay Mandal**

('Victory Tower'). The view
from the top gives you a
good idea of the extent of
the site.

Mohammad-bin-Tughlaq
succeeded his father five
years after the completion
of the city, but in true Tughlaq fashion decided that he
had to build a city of his
own, and moved everyone
out, so Tughlaqabad was
occupied for a far shorter
period of time than it took
to build.

The Tughlaqabad site is
huge and feels rather remote.
Women on their own should
take great care as there have
been some unpleasant inci-
dents here.

On the opposite side of
the Mehrauli–Badarpur Road
to the south of the walled city
stands Ghazi Malik's tomb,
originally in the centre of a
lake (now dry) and connected
to the city via a causeway.
The high esteem in which the
city's founder was held is
reflected in the use of sandstone to build his final resting
place, rather than the
cheaper local stone used
elsewhere.
SEE ALSO MONUMENTS, P.83

57

History

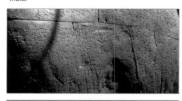

300BC
Earliest archaeological evidence of settlement in Delhi area.

268–232
Mauryan emperor Ashoka rules over much of North India.

AD275–550
The Gupta empire controls North India.

AD700–1150
The Tomar Rajputs rule Delhi.

1151–92
The Chauhan Rajputs take over from the Tomars.

1191
Rai Pithora Chauhan crushes Mohammad-bin-Sam at first battle of Tarain.

1192
Second battle of Tarain. Chauhan is killed. Qutb-ud-din Aibak becomes governor of Delhi (sultan from 1206). Beginning of the Delhi Sultanates.

1211
Iltutmish becomes sultan. Completes the Qutb Minar.

1296–1316
Reign of Ala-ud-din. Construction of Siri Fort.

1320S
Ghazi Malik builds Tughlaqabad.

1354
Feroz Shah Tughlaq builds Ferozabad.

1398
Delhi taken by Tamerlane.

1414–51
The Sayyid dynasty rule Delhi.

1451–1526
The Lodis take over rule of city.

1526
Babur invades India and defeats Ibrahim Lodi at battle of Panipat. Beginning of Mughal dynasty.

1530
Humayun comes to the throne; exiled by Sher Shah in 1539.

1555
Humayun regains power.

1556
Humayun dies from falling down steps of library in Purana Qila.

1556–1605
Reign of Akbar.

1638
Shah Jahan begins building Shahjahanabad, including Lal Qila and Jama Masjid.

1658–1707
Reign of Aurangzeb.

1739
Nadir Shah sacks Delhi; takes Peacock Throne.

1803
Establishment of East India Company rule.

1857
The Great Uprising ('Indian Mutiny'). End of Mughal rule. British Crown takes over administration, with Calcutta (Kolkata) as capital.

1866
Railways come to Delhi.

1877
Queen Victoria made empress of India.

1911
Delhi Durbar. Announcement that Delhi is to become capital of India.

1947
Independence, Jawaharlal Nehru becomes prime minister. Country partitioned into India and Pakistan. 10 million people migrate and between 200,000 and 1 million are killed.

1948
Mahatma Gandhi is assassinated in Delhi.

1951
India becomes a republic. First general elections.

1984
Sikhs demand independence for Punjab. Indira Gandhi assassinated in Delhi, anti-Sikh riots sweep the city.

1991
Rajiv Gandhi is assassinated.

2002
First line of metro system opened.

2003
Delhi announced as host of the 2010 Commonwealth Games.

2004
Congress under Man Mohan Singh win general election.

2005
Delhi's population crosses 15 million mark.

2008
Bombs explode across the capital killing over 30 people.

2010
After a shaky start, the Commonwealth Games pass off reasonably well, only to be followed by a high-profile inquest into corruption during the preparations.

59

Hotels

In terms of places to stay Delhi has just about everything, from the worst fleapits imaginable (none of which are listed here) to some of the most luxurious hotels in the country. While some of the top-end places are identical to those found all over the world, a new and very welcome trend has been the emergence of both funky and chic design hotels. As well as some charming lower-key places that have a more 'Indian' feel than the large five-stars, there are now an increasing number of 'home stays' setting up, where visitors can find accommodation with local families.

Connaught Place

Choudhary Guest House
H 35/3 Connaught Place; tel: 4350 9878; www.indiamart.com/hkchoudharyguesthouse; £; metro: Rajiv Chowk; map p.137 C4

This small, clean and friendly hotel is one of the best of the cheaper options in the centre. It has a great location, and an exceptionally helpful manager, but it can be a struggle to find – it's very tucked away, but well worth tracking down.

Imperial Hotel
1 Janpath; tel: 2334 1234; www.theimperialindia.com; £££££; metro: Rajiv Chowk; map p.137 C4

Pretty much as good as it gets in Delhi, this place oozes class and Art Deco charm in equal measure. Built

Prices for a standard double room, including breakfast, in high season:
£ under Rs 1,500
££ Rs 1,500–3,000
£££ Rs 3,000–6,000
££££ Rs 6,000–10,000
£££££ over Rs 10,000

in 1933, it was the only hotel included in Lutyens's plans for New Delhi. The entrance drive is flanked by huge palm trees, behind which is the pool. The rooms are decorated with lithographs and engravings from the owner's private collection, and it has one of Delhi's best restaurants (**The Spice Route**).
SEE ALSO RESTAURANTS, P.113

Marina Radisson
G59 Connaught Circus; tel: 4690 9090; www.radisson.com; £££££; metro: Rajiv Chowk; map p.137 C4

Recently renovated hotel in a heritage building right in the heart of town. Rooms offer all the standard five-star comforts, and with so many of Delhi's attractions within easy reach this makes a good choice.

Master Paying Guest House
R-500 New Rajendar Nagar; tel: 2874 1089; www.masterguesthouse.com; ££; metro: Rajendra Place; map p.134 A1

Small and sweet, with only four very clean and comfortable rooms with a shared bathroom. The guesthouse is

Many of the most luxurious hotels in Delhi can be found just south of Connaught Place (a good hunting ground for design hotels) and in the Diplomatic Enclave in Chanakyapuri. If you are looking for something less corporate, then the area around Lodi Gardens and South Delhi have some lovely smaller hotels. Most of the city's homestays can be found, not surprisingly, in the residential colonies to the northwest and south. Further out, in Gurgaon and towards Delhi's airports, are some impressive luxury business hotels.

run by a very helpful couple, and there is a nice common area including a TV and a library created by the guests.

The Metropolitan
Bangla Sahib Road; tel: 4250 0200; www.hotelmetdelhi.com; £££££; metro: R.K. Ashram Marg; map p.136 C4

Although it is exceptionally well run and well equipped for the business traveller, this is perhaps a little more faceless than some of the other five-stars nearby and fairly

Left: the Art Deco Imperial Hotel in New Delhi is set in beautiful gardens.

guesthouse in a modern family home. There is a pleasant veranda overlooking the small garden and a courtyard to eat in. Near to Connaught Place, this is one of the quietest options so close to town.

YWCA International Guest House

10 Sansad Marg; tel: 2336 1662; www.ywcaindia.org; ££; metro: Patel Chowk; map p.137 C4

A well-run and safe place to stay for both sexes, in a convenient New Delhi location. The spotless air-conditioned rooms with attached bath come with a complimentary breakfast at a good restaurant (**Ten**) on the ground floor of the building. The profits go towards projects helping women in India.

SEE ALSO RESTAURANTS, P.113

Old Delhi and Raj Ghat

Hotel Broadway

4/15A Asaf Ali Road; tel: 4366 3600; www.oldworldhospitality. com; £££; metro: New Delhi; map p.135 D2

A long-standing and good-value hotel close to the sights of Old Delhi. The lovely rooms have recently been given a make-over, the

expensive. On the plus side, there is a good health spa and the best Japanese restaurant in town bar none (**Sakura**).

SEE ALSO RESTAURANTS, P.113

The Park

15 Sansad Marg; tel: 2374 3000; www.theparkhotels.com; £££££; metro: Rajiv Chowk; map p.137 C4

The Park pioneered the design hotel concept in India and they remain some of the best. Perhaps the funkiest contemporary-style rooms in town, plus an interesting restaurant, poolside bar (**Aqua**) and great location make this a winner. **Agni**, the hotel's DJ bar is one of the liveliest in town.

SEE ALSO CAFÉS AND BARS, P.28

Shangri-La Hotel

19 Ashoka Road; tel: 4119 1919; www.shangri-la.com; £££££; metro: Patel Chowk; map p.137 C3

This relatively new addition to central Delhi's luxury hotels is a real stunner. Not only do the public areas exude class,

it has beautifully designed and extremely comfortable rooms and can also boast of having one of the best East Asian restaurants in the city (**19 Oriental Avenue**). A great spa and swimming pool, plus a couple of very cool bars round off the picture.

SEE ALSO PAMPERING, P.97; RESTAURANTS, P.112

Yatri House

3–4 Panchkuian Marg; tel: 2362 5563; www.yatrihouse.com; £££; metro: R.K. Ashram Marg; map p.134 C2

Down a small lane, well set back from the busy main road, this is a clean, well-run

Right: designer touch at a Delhi hotel.

61

service is good, and it has an excellent restaurant (the **Chor Bizarre**).

SEE ALSO RESTAURANTS, P.114

North Delhi

Bajaj Indian Home Stay
8A/34 WEA, Karol Bagh;
tel: 2573 6509; www.bajaj indianhomestay.com; £££;
metro: Karol Bagh;
map p.134 B2

Promising an experience that's 'Indian, altogether', this place prides itself on its homely ambience, treating each guest as one of its own. With 10 rooms it is a little bigger than the usual 'home stay', but it still stands out from the crowd, and the rooms are spotlessly clean. Although to the north of the city it is not very far from Connaught Place.

Good Times Hotel
8/7 WEA Karol Bagh, opposite Ramjas School, Pusa Road;
tel: 4154 4444; www.goodtimes hotel.com; £££; metro: Rajendra Place; map p.134 A2

Presentable rooms and a pleasant rooftop restaurant just about make up for the busy, if fairly convenient,

location. The staff seem rushed off their feet most of the time. This is one of the better-value places around, so book early.

Maiden's Hotel
7 Sham Nath Marg; tel: 2397 5464; www.maidenshotel.com; £££££; metro: Civil Lines; map p.135 D4

A grand hotel in the Civil Lines close to Old Delhi – built during the 1900s – and before Lutyens's redevelopment a favourite with visiting bigwigs. The large rooms and attentive service are lovely and not as expensive as you might imagine. The

The price guides given here are correct at the time of going to press, and include the government luxury tax of 12.5 percent. However, it is thought there is a shortage of rooms in the city, so it is likely that prices for accommodation in Delhi will continue to rise. Check the hotels' websites for latest prices and do keep an eye out for special offers, some of which can be very reasonable.

Curzon Room restaurant serves very good food from the British Raj.

Rajpath and Chanakyapuri

The Claridges
12 Aurangzeb Road; tel: 3955 5000; www.claridges.com; £££££; metro: Udyog Bhavan; map p.137 C2

A refined hotel in the heart of New Delhi. The rooms have an understated elegance and are very comfortable, and the service is excellent. There are also a couple of good restaurants (Punjabi food at the **Dhaba** and Mediterranean at the **Sevilla**). The **Aura** bar is one of the best, and most sophisticated, places in the city for a drink.

SEE ALSO CAFÉS AND BARS, P.29

Hotel Diplomat
9 Sardar Patel Marg, Chanakyapuri; tel: 2301 0204; www.the hoteldiplomat.com; £££££; metro: Central Secretariat; map p.136 A2

Right: elegant and comfortable rooms behind the Art Deco façade of the Vivanti by Taj – Ambassador, *see p.65.*

Left: alfresco breakfast and comfy beds at The Claridges.

A quiet hotel with a pleasant garden. The elegant, Modernist rooms with large windows are popular and advance booking is advisable, not least as the prices are reasonable compared to other top hotels in the city. The Diplomat has undergone a renaissance of late, not least as it is the location of the über trendy **Olive Beach** restaurant.

ITC Maurya
Sardar Patel Marg, Chanakyapuri; tel: 2611 2233; www. itcwelcom group.in; £££££; metro: Dhaula Kuan; map p.136 A2

Like the Taj Palace *(see p.63)*, this highly luxurious hotel not only attracts the travelling 'great and good' but also scores on account of its two fabulous Indian restaurants, the **Bukhara** and the **Dum Phukt**. Cheap? No (it's one of the most expensive places in Delhi), but the service and rooms are second to none.

Prices for a standard double room, including breakfast, in high season:
£ under Rs 1,500
££ Rs 1,500–3,000
£££ Rs 3,000–6,000
££££ Rs 6,000–10,000
£££££ over Rs 10,000

Jukaso Inn
50 Sunder Nagar; tel: 2435 0308; www.jukasohotels.com; ££££; metro: Khan Market; map p.137 E2

Located in one of Delhi's most desirable residential areas, this is the biggest and best of the several hotels in the area. The 33 rooms are well kept if a little pricey for the amenities, but the staff go out of their way to please. Book well in advance.

Leela Palace Kempinski
1 Mansingh Road; tel: 2302 6162; www.tajhotels.com; £££££; metro: Khan Market; map p.137 D2

A brand new addition to Delhi's five-star scene, this is an impressively lavish hotel in a superb location.

The rooms are exquisitely opulent, and the restaurants and public spaces exude class, meaning this should soon be seen as one of Delhi's top hotels.

Taj Mahal
1 Mansingh Road; tel: 2302 6162; www.tajhotels.com; £££££; metro: Khan Market; map p.137 D2

The impressive flagship of the Taj Group is primarily a business hotel and the well-appointed rooms and facilities reflect this. It also has some very good restaurants (the **Machan**, great for its buffet lunch, the Chinese **House of Ming** and the excellent **Wasabi**). The hotel's bar, **Ricks**, mixes some of the best cocktails in Delhi.

SEE ALSO CAFÉS AND BARS, P.30; RESTAURANTS, P.116

Taj Palace
Sardar Patel Marg, Chanakyapuri; tel: 2611 0202; www.tajhotels. com; £££££; metro: Dhaula Kuan; map p.136 A2

While its luxurious suites are much loved by visiting dignitaries (not least because of

its easy access from the airport and location in the heart of diplomat-land), this well-designed hotel caters for all visitors and sits in beautiful grounds. Its star attractions, however, are its restaurants (**Masala Art** and **Orient Express**), among the very best in Delhi.
SEE ALSO RESTAURANTS, P.115, 116

Youth Hostel
5 Nyaya Marg, Chanakyapuri; tel: 2611 6285; www.hihostels. com; £; metro: Udyog Bhavan; map p.136 B2
A large, modern and good-value hostel, set in the pleasant diplomatic quarter. You must be a member of Hostelling International to stay here (there is a wide network of hostels in India, so you might want to take out membership before you travel; see the website above for details).

Lodi Gardens and Nizamuddin

Ahuja Residency
193 Golf Links; tel: 2462 2255; www.ahujaresidency.com; £££; metro: Khan Market; map p.137 D2
Clean, friendly, quiet and relaxing, this well-located guesthouse is one of Delhi's hidden gems. Great value

If you intend to make your stay in Delhi more of a shopping and pampering excursion than anything then certain hotels will be more convenient – and chic – than others. Try The Aman near Khan and Lodi Markets; The Park, Hans and Shangri-La are all good for Connaught Place; or check out the Amarya guesthouses and The Manor in South Delhi.

to boot; make sure you book well in advance. The owners have another, smaller and slightly cheaper, property in Defence Colony a short distance away, plus a new property in Sunder Nagar.

The Aman
Lodi Road, Nizamuddin West; tel: 4363 3333; www.aman resorts.com; £££££; metro: JLN Stadium; map p.137 D2
Although only a few years old, this very chic designer hotel is now one of the city's finest. With local stone floors and *jali* screens, it aims at a contemporary Indian ambience. A place to stay and pamper yourself, not only do most of the rooms and suites (some of which are truly luxurious) have their own private plunge-pools, but the hotel has a state-of-the-art spa.

Right: the trendy Threesixty, *see p.117*, at the Oberoi.

Jorbagh 27
27 Jorbagh; tel: 2469 4430; www.jorbagh27.com; £££; metro: Jor Bagh; map p.137 C1
Set in a residential area, but run more as a hotel than a guesthouse, this 18-room property lacks some of the charm of the more homely establishments, but is efficiently run, clean and well located, with the proximity of Lodi Gardens a real bonus.

Lutyens Bungalow
39 Prithviraj Road; tel: 2461 1341; www.lutyensbungalow. co.in; ££££; metro: Race Course; map p.137 C2
Set in a Lutyens-designed bungalow on one of the capital's most exclusive roads, this 15-room guesthouse retains the building's original charm, has a very friendly but unobtrusive feel and a swimming pool in the lovely gardens. A real chance to experience part of New Delhi's history at first hand; be sure to book well in advance.

Oberoi
Dr Zakir Hussain Marg; tel: 2436 3030; www.oberoihotels.com; £££££; metro: JLN Stadium; map p.137 D2
Once the standard bearer for Delhi's five-star hotels, the

Oberoi is still elegant, exclusive and very expensive. One of the most comfortable luxury hotels in the city, its rooms have spectacular views and a traditional feel. As well as a great spa and the justly famous pool, the hotel's **Threesixty** restaurant is one of the trendiest, and most accomplished places in town.

Vivanta by Taj - Ambassador
Sujan Singh Park, Subramaniam Bharti Marg; tel: 6626 1000; www.vivantabytaj.com/ambassador-new-delhi; ££££; metro: Khan Market; map p.137 D2

A Taj-run, slightly old-fashioned hotel near Khan Market that has been given a face lift since becoming part of the Vivanta chain. Comfortable and not as overpowering as the Taj Mahal or Taj Palace *(see p.63)* – and cheaper – it is a nicely laid-back place to stay. If you can get them, the rooms overlooking the Art Deco façade have large balconies. The undersea-themed **H20+** bar is good for a drink.

Left: elements of the Lutyens Bungalow.

South Delhi

Amarya Garden
C-179 Defence Colony; tel: 4656 2735; www.amaryagroup.com; ££££; metro: Lajpath Nagar; map p.139 D4

This wonderful little boutique hotel is the second of the small French-run Amarya guesthouses to open in the city. In a great location and with just four beautifully decorated rooms, all very minimal and *très chic*, once you throw in the lovely garden and decent food it all adds up to one of the best places to stay in Delhi.

Amarya Haveli
P5 Hauz Khas Enclave; tel: 4175 9268; www.amaryagroup.com; ££££; metro: Green Park; map p.138 C3

Sister hotel to the Amarya Garden *(above)* just a bit further out in the attractive Hauz Khas district. There is the same attention to detail, contemporary Indian décor and good food on offer. It is a fraction cheaper than the Garden but an equally good choice. A third property, Amarya Villa (tel: 4175 9267) in Safdarjung Enclave, is now open for business.

Chirag
B-18 Chirag Enclave; tel: 4954 1111; www.chiragboutique hotel.com; £££; metro: Nehru Place; map p.139 E3

One of the better choices in this price range, if not quite as boutique as it makes out. The rooms are clean and well appointed, and with the addition of the metro Nehru Place has become quite a desirable area, making this a good value option.

Delhi Bed and Breakfast
A-6 Friend's Colony East; tel: 981 105 7103; www.delhibedand breakfast.com; £££; metro: Lajpath Nagar

Not to be confused with the New Delhi B&B *(see p.67)*, this friendly home stay has a really Indian feel to it, in the best possible sense. Set in a great family house, it is a

> Prices for a standard double room, including breakfast, in high season:
> £ under Rs 1,500
> ££ Rs 1,500–3,000
> £££ Rs 3,000–6,000
> ££££ Rs 6,000–10,000
> £££££ over Rs 10,000

Left: outside seating at the Lutyens Bungalow, *see p.64.*

Vasant Continental

Basant Lok, Vasant Vihar; tel: 2614 8800; www.jaypee hotels. com; £££££; metro: Hauz Khas; map p.138 A3

From a stable of business hotels, this luxury outfit's contemporary styling makes it stand out. Comfortable and close to the airport in an up-market residential area, it has a good pool, a lively bar and good food. The more central sister hotel, the Siddarth, at 3 Rajendra Place, is just as well run, and has a wonderful pool and a pleasant bar, **Tapas**.

Mehrauli and Tughlaqabad

The Grand

Nelson Mandela Road, Vasant Kunj; tel: 2677 1234; www.the grandnewdelhi.com; £££££; metro: Hauz Khas

Although not as self-consciously cool as the Galaxy *(see below)*, The Grand's classy, contemporary design helps this property stand out from the rest of the five-stars near the airport. If you have just flown in, or are on your way out, it is convenient, comfortable and has a good range of restaurants

perfect retreat from busy Delhi streets, and the owners are a mine of information about the city and surrounding areas. The home-cooked food is particulary delicious.

Hyatt Regency

Bhikaiji Cama Place, Ring Road; tel: 2679 1234; www.delhi. regency.hyatt.com; £££££; metro: INA; map p.138 B4

What's big and swish and found on the Ring Road? Answer, the Hyatt Regency. Not a shrinking violet this one; the impressive bulk of the exterior prepares you for the equally brash lobby. The rooms, while aimed at business travellers, have a cool, contemporary feel.

The Manor

77 Friends Colony West; tel: 2692 5151; www.themanor delhi.com; ££££; metro: Jang-pura; map p.139 E4

One of Delhi's most sleek and attractive luxury places

to stay. Twelve nicely thought-out rooms, with lots of natural fabrics and wonderful bathrooms. Although it might lack the facilities (such as a pool) of the large five-stars, it does have a beautiful garden and makes a wonderfully quiet and discreet place to stay. The rates for the standard rooms are surprisingly good.

Thikana

A-7 Gulmohar Park; tel: 4604 1569; www.thikanadelhi.com; £££; metro: Green Park; map p.139 C3

A lovely modern guesthouse, small without being cloying; there are seven rooms, all well decorated and with good en suite bathrooms. It has a more contemporary feel than some home stays (Wi-fi and DVDs), and the owners are helpful and very friendly, dishing up a great breakfast.

The city's home-stay pro-gramme was launched by Delhi Tourism in 2007, encouraging local people to open up their houses as bed & breakfast accommodation. A full list of officially sanctioned places can be seen at www.delhitourism. nic.in. It has been so successful that larger operators are now getting involved, the most prominent being Mahindra, which has properties in South Extension and Gurgaon (for more details see www. mahindrahomestays.com).

Prices for a standard double room, including breakfast, in high season:
£ under Rs 1,500
££ Rs 1,500–3,000
£££ Rs 3,000–6,000
££££ Rs 6,000–10,000
£££££ over Rs 10,000

and a bar. As a bonus it has a good pool and a spa, as well as very helpful staff.

New Delhi Bed & Breakfast
C8/8225 Vasant Kunj; tel: 2689 4812; www.newdelhibedand breakfast.com; ££–£££; metro: Hauz Khas

A little way out of the centre, between the airport and Qutb Minar, this is an attractive and quiet home stay. With only two rooms (decorated in blue or yellow), it has a homely and friendly atmosphere, and the small patio where you can sit out is an added attraction. With good rates and a tasty breakfast as part of the package, this is a good option if you want to be this side of town.

Gurgaon and Noida

Galaxy
NH-8, Sector 15, Part II, Gurgaon; tel: 0124-486 8000; www.galaxyhotel.in; £££££; metro: Gurgaon

This contemporary luxury hotel is handy for the airport as well as being a good place to stay if you want a modern design hotel in the 'New India' that is Gurgaon (an experience in itself). The rooms are minimally chic with great bathrooms, and very comfortable. Better still, it has a great spa with a rooftop swimming pool, and a classy bar/restaurant (**Terroir**) with decent wines and good pan-European food.

Right: effortless elegance at The Manor.

Lemon Tree Hotel
287 Millenium City Center, Sector 29, Gurgaon, tel: 0124 416 0303; www.lemontreehotels.com; £££–££££; metro: Gurgaon

Efficient, modern hotel from this fast expanding chain which has successfully catered to the business and leisure crowd looking for moderately priced but well-maintained accommodation below the five-star bracket. No frills or character as such, but dependable and reasonable.

Trident
443 Udyog Vihar, Phase V, Gurgaon; tel: 0124-245 0505; www.tridenthotels.com; £££££; metro: Gurgaon

Said by some to be India's best business hotel, and it is certainly one of the most expensive, the Trident is lavish, designed to within an inch of its life, and has an amazing swimming pool. Is it worth the money (currently around Rs 20,000 for the cheapest double)? Probably, for the top-class business services it offers, if you want to be in Gurgaon and are in need of pampering. If it is design and convenience you are after, then The Aman and The Park give it some serious competition and are considerably more at the centre of things.

67

Language

With 18 official languages, hundreds of others and countless dialects, India can present a linguistic minefield. Luckily for the traveller, English is often understood, and it is usually possible to get by. However, attempts to speak the local language are always appreciated. The language most widely spoken in Delhi is Hindi, along with its close relation Urdu and Punjabi. Hindi is written in the Devanagiri script (with the bar running across the top of the characters), also used for Sanskrit, and Punjabi in the related Gurmukhi. Urdu, spoken mostly in Old Delhi, uses a flowing Persian script.

Pronunciation

Indian languages are phonetically regular, based on syllables rather than an alphabet. Important differences are made between long and short vowels, and retroflex, palatal and labial consonants; listen hard, or ask a native speaker, to get a feel for the vocabulary below. There are various systems of transliteration, and you may see many of the words below spelt different ways in English. Where a consonant is followed by 'h' this is an aspirated sound, and 'c' is usually pronounced 'ch' (followed by 'h', 'chh').

Basic Hindi

Hello/goodbye *Namaste*
Yes *Ji ha*
No *Ji nehi*
Perhaps *Shayad*
Thank you *Dhanyavad/shukriya*
How are you? *Ap kaise hai?/Ap thik hai?*
I am well *Me thik hu/thik hai*
What is your name? *Apka nam kya hai?*
My name is (John/Jane) *Mera nam (John/Jane) hai*
Where do you come from? *Ap kahan se aye?*
From (England) *(England) se*
How much (money)? *Kitna paise hai?*
That is expensive *Bahut mahenga hai*
Cheap *Sasta*
I like (tea) *Mujhe (chai) pasand hai*
Is it possible? *Kya ye sambhav hai?*
I don't understand *Mujhe samajh nehi*
I don't know *Mujhe malum nehi*
Money *Paisa*
Newspaper *Akhbar*
Blanket *Kambal*
Bed *Palang*
Room *Kamra*
Please clean my room *Mera kamra saf kijie*
Clothes *Kapre*
Cloth *Kapra*
Market *Bajar*

Pronouns and Verbs

I am *Mai hun*
You are *Ap hain*
He/she/it is *Voh hai*
They are *Ve hain*
To drink *Pina*
To eat *Khanna*
To do/make *Karna*
To buy *Kharidna*
To sleep *Sona*
To see *Dekhna*
To hear/listen to *Sunna*
To wash (clothes) *Dhona*
To wash (yourself) *Nahana*
To get *Milna/pana*

Prepositions, Adverbs and Adjectives

Now *Ab*
Right now *Abhi*
Quickly *Jaldi*
Slowly *Dirhe se*
A lot *Bahut*
A little *Tora*
Here *Yaha/idhar*
There *Vaha/udhar*
Open *Khola*
Closed *Band*
Finished *Khatam hai*
Big/older *Bara*
Small/younger *Chota*
Beautiful *Sundar*
Old *Purana*
New *Naya*

Questions

What is? *Kya hai?*
Where is? *Kahan hai?*
Why? *Kyun?*
Who is? *Kaun hai?*
When is? *Kab hai?*
How? *Kaisa?*

Left: bilingual metro sign.

ulti ho rahi thi
I have a temperature *Mujhe bukhar hai*
I have a headache *Mere sir men dard hai*
I have a stomach ache *Mere pat men dard hai*
I have diarrhoea *Mujhe dast ar raha hai*
The English word 'motions' is a common expression for diarrhoea.

Travel

Where is (Delhi)? *(Dilli) kahan hai?*
Bus station *Bus adda*
Railway station *Tren stashan/railgari*
Airport *Hawai adda*
Car *Gari*
How far is it? *Kitni dur hai?*
In front of/opposite (the Lal Qila) *(Lal Qila) ke samne*
Near *Ke nazdik/ke pas*
Far *Dur*
Stop *Rukh jaiye*
Let's go *Chele jao*
I have to go *Mujhe jana hai*
Come *Ayie*
Go *Jayie*

Numbers

1 *ek*
2 *do*
3 *tin*
4 *char*
5 *panch*
6 *che*
7 *sat*
8 *arth*
9 *nau*
10 *das*
20 *bis*
30 *tis*
40 *chalis*
50 *pachas*
60 *sath*
70 *setur*
80 *assi*
90 *nabbe*
100 *sau*
1,000 *hazar*
100,000 *lakh*
10,000,000 *kror*

Most straightforward sentences can easily be turned into a question by putting '*kya*' on the front and raising the pitch of the voice at the end of the sentence, e.g. *'Dhobi hai'*, 'There is a washerman', *'Kya dhobi hai?'* 'There is a washerman?'

Days and Months

Monday *Somvar*
Tuesday *Mangalvar*
Wednesday *Budhvar*
Thursday *Guruvar*
Friday *Shukravar*
Saturday *Shanivar*
Sunday *Itvar*
Today *Aj*
Yesterday/tomorrow *kal*
Week *Hafta*
January *Janvari*
February *Farvari*
March *March*
April *Aprail*
May *Mai*
June *Jun*
July *Julai*
August *Agast*
September *Sitambar*
October *Aktubar*
November *Navambar*
December *Disambar*
Month *Mahina*
Year *Sal*

Relatives

Mother *Mata-ji*
Father *Pita-ji*
Sister *Behen*
Brother *Bhai*
Husband *Pati*
Wife *Patni*
Maternal grandmother *Nani*
Maternal grandfather *Nana*
Paternal grandmother *Dadi*
Paternal grandfather *Dada*
Elder sister (term of respect) *Didi*
Daughter *Beti*
Son *Beta*
Girl *Larki*
Boy *Larka*
Are you married? *Kya ap shadishuda hai?*
Are you single (male/female)? *Kya ap akela/akeli?*
How many children have you got? *Apke kitne bache hai?*
How many brothers and sisters have you got? *Apke kitne bhai behen hai?*

Health

Doctor *Daktar*
Hospital *Aspatal*
Dentist *Dentist*
Pain *Dard*
I am ill *Main bimar hun*
I have been vomiting *Mujhe*

Literature and Theatre

India has a strong literary tradition, and a number of its contemporary novelists have achieved international fame, with Aravind Adiga winning the 2008 Booker Prize for his first novel (other Indian winners include Salman Rushdie and Arundati Roy). The country has a thriving publishing industry and Delhi is an excellent – and cheap – place to buy books. Delhi's literary preoccupation continues into a lively local theatre scene, but perhaps even more interesting are the performances of traditional dramas.

Suggested Reading

DESIGN

India Contemporary
by **Henry Wilson** (Thames & Hudson, 2007). The photographer turns his eye to the modern homes of India's elite; beautiful images show off the eclectic fusion of contemporary design with Indian motifs.
India: Decoration, Interiors, Style
by **Henry Wilson** (Conran-

India has three national bookshop chains, selling everything from blockbusters to textbooks, all with modern interiors and with most branches having an in-store café. **Crossword** (www.crosswordbookstores.com; daily 11am–9pm) can be found at Select Citywalk and the Metropolitan malls, both in Saket, South Delhi. The **Oxford Bookstore** (www.oxfordbookstore.com; daily 10am–8.30pm) is more central, and is located in Statesman House, Connaught Place, while Odyssey (www.odyssey.in) has outlets at many of the metro stations and at 18A Khan Market.

Octopus, 2006). Exquisite photography of a number of North Indian palaces and houses, demonstrating the inventiveness and sense of design to be found in this part of India.
Mansions at Dusk: the Havelis of Old Delhi
by **Pavan K. Varma** (Spantech, 1992). Atmospheric photographs by Sondeep Shankar illustrate this homage to the now decaying mansions of Muslim Delhi.

FICTION

Bunker 13
by **Anirudha Bahal** (Faber & Faber, 2004). Derring-do, double crosses and drugs on the Kashmir border, mixed in with the wild side of modern Delhi.
Clear Light of Day
by **Anita Desai** (Penguin, 1982). The difficulties of post-Partition India seen through the eyes of a Hindu family living in Old Delhi.
Delhi, A Novel
by **Kushwant Singh** (Viking, 1989). A bawdy saga that takes us through 600 years of temptresses and traitors to unravel the Indian capital's

mystique. Narrated in turns by a eunuch, an irreverent wag, potentates and poets. Superb. (It took this popular author 20 years to write.)
In Custody
by **Anita Desai** (Heinemann, 1984). The last days of an Urdu poet in Old Delhi.
One Night at the Call Centre
by **Chetan Bhagat** (Black Swan, 2007). Bhagat's comedies of young middle-class Indian life have taken Delhi by storm, much to the disapproval of some in the literary world. This and his previous book, *Five Point Someone* (Rupa, 2006), give one of the best introductions to how this very visible part of Delhi's population lives and thinks.
Red Earth and Pouring Rain
by **Vikram Chandra** (Viking, 1996). Acclaimed debut novel, quick-paced and audacious.
Sea of Poppies
by **Amitav Ghosh** (John Murray, 2008). This hard-hitting novel is set in the Ghaziabad opium factory from where the British exported the drug to China.

Left: at Full Circle, *see p.73.*

The Discovery of India
by **Jawaharlal Nehru** (Asia Publishing House, 1966). Revealing history by India's first prime minister, which tells as much about the author as its subject.

Freedom at Midnight
by **Larry Collins and Dominique Lapierre** (Tarang, 1975). Gripping popular history of the birth of the Indian nation.

The Great Moghuls
by **Bamber Gascoigne** (Cape, 1971). Well-researched book which describes the dynasty that for two centuries ruled India, in turn both enlightened and decadent, austere and brutal.

A History of India, Volume I
by **Romila Thapar** (Pelican, 2003). Second edition of this highly acclaimed history. Volume 1 traces the history of South Asia from ancient times through to the Delhi Sultanate. Volume II, by **Perceval Spear**, continues from the Mughals to the assassination of M.K. Gandhi.

India: a History
by **John Keay** (HarperCollins, 2000). A one-volume history by a well-respected writer. Also by Keay, *India Discovered* (Collins, 1998) documents the unearthing of India's past by British scholars and adventurers.

The Last Mughal
by **William Dalrymple**

A Suitable Boy
by **Vikram Seth** (Phoenix Press, 1994). A multi-faceted novel set during the run-up to Independent India's first elections, which centres around a mother's search for a suitable husband for her daughter.

Train to Pakistan
by **Kushwant Singh** (various editions, 1975). Gripping story of the excesses of Partition.

Transmission
by **Hari Kunzru** (Penguin, 2005). The amusing story of Arjun Mehta, an ex-pat IT worker in the US who wreaks his revenge on the system.

The White Tiger
by **Aravind Adiga** (Atlantic Books, 2008). Booker Prize-winning first novel that exposes the underbelly of modern India.

Women Writing in India: 600BC to the Present
ed. **Susie Tharu and K. Lalitha** (Feminist Press, 1991). Wonderful and eclectic anthology bringing to light the neglected history of Indian women. Volume 1 includes writings from 600 BC to the early 20th century; volume 2 concentrates on the 20th century alone.

Yaarana: Gay Writing from India
ed. **Hoshang Merchant**, and *Facing the Mirror: Lesbian Writing from India*, ed. **Ashwini Sukthankar** (both Penguin, 1999). Anthologies of short stories, extracts from novels and poetry from gay and lesbian Indian writers.

HISTORY
An Autobiography, or My Experiments with Truth
by **M.K. Gandhi** (Penguin, 1982). A translation from the original Gujarati which shows the complex and at times flawed nature of one of India's greatest popular leaders.

Right: Bahri Sons in Khan Market, *see p.72.*

(Penguin, 2006). Dalrymple recounts the story of Bahadur Shah and the 1857 Uprising.

Liberty or Death: India's Journey to Independence and Division
by **Patrick French** (Harper-Collins, 1997). Readable, well-researched account of the freedom struggle and Partition.

The Nehrus and the Gandhis: an Indian Dynasty
by **Tariq Ali** (Pan, 1985). A gripping account of India's famous political family. Recently reprinted in India.

No Full Stops in India
by **Mark Tully** (Viking, 1991). Essays on modern political India by the BBC's ex-South Asia correspondent.

LANGUAGE

Hanklyn-Janklin, or a Stranger's Rumble Tumble Guide to some Words, Customs and Quiddities Indian and Indo-British
by **Nigel B. Hankin** (Banyan Books, 1992). Lives up to its title and is a delightful reference work.

Hobson-Jobson
by **Henry Yule** (Routledge and Kegan Paul, 1968). The 1886 glossary on which Hankin modelled his modern etymology.

SOCIETY, CULTURE AND RELIGION

The Argumentative Indian
by **Amartya Sen** (Penguin, 2006). Reflections on culture, history and identity by India's Nobel Prize-winner.

Gods, Demons and Others
by **R.K. Narayan** (Heinemann, 1986). Retellings of some of India's most popular religious myths by one of the country's greatest writers. Also worth looking out for are his retellings of the *Ramayana* (Penguin, 1977), based on the Tamil Kamban version, and the *Mahabharata* (Heinemann, 1986).

The Idea of India
by **Sunil Khilnani** (Hamish Hamilton, 1997). Intellectual tour de force examines concepts about an ancient civilisation and its status as a relatively new nation.

In Spite of the Gods
by **Edward Luce** (Abacus, 2006). A searching dissection of modern India – its politics, economics and future direction – by the India correspondent of the *Financial Times*.

Indira: the Life of Indira Nehru Gandhi
by **Katherine Frank** (Harper-Collins, 2002). An in-depth biography of one of post-Independence India's most charismatic leaders.

Intimate Relations: Exploring Indian Sexuality
by **Sudhir Kakar** (University of Chicago Press, 1990). This study throws light on many aspects of Indian marital and family relations.

A Million Mutinies Now
by **V.S. Naipul** (Heinemann, 1990). The misanthropic scholar returns to seek his roots and finds a cast of characters not easily pigeon-holed. A positive follow-up to his jaundiced **India: A Wounded**

Civilisation (Penguin, 1979).

The Other Side of Silence: Voices from the Partition of India
by **Urvashi Butalia** (Penguin, 1998). Tales of families torn apart for 50 years, compellingly told by India's leading literary feminist.

Temptations of the West, or How to be Modern in India, Pakistan and Beyond
by **Pankaj Mishra** (Picador, 2006). An insightful account of the dilemmas faced by modern India by the author of *Butter Chicken in Ludhiana*.

TRAVEL

Butter Chicken in Ludhiana: Travels in Small Town India
by **Pankaj Mishra** (Penguin, 1995). An urban Indian novelist casts a jaundiced eye over the emerging middle class during the 1990s. Still relevant and very amusing.

City of Djinns
by **William Dalrymple** (HarperCollins, 1993). The respected travel writer's account of a year spent in Delhi, full of historical references.

Delhi, Adventures in a Megacity by **Sam Miller** (Penguin/Viking, 2008). Account of a spiralling walk round Delhi, taking in some of the less well-known areas, full of interesting anecdotes and discoveries.

Bookshops

Bahri Sons
Opposite Main Gate, Khan Market; tel: 2469 4610; www.books atbahri.com; Mon–Sat 10.30am–7.30pm; metro: Khan Market; map p. 137 D2
A long-standing bookshop with an impressive range of titles.

The Bookshop
13/7 Jor Bagh Market; tel: 2469

Left: India illustrated.

Left: the bookshelves at the Jawaharlal Nehru Memorial Museum, *see p.88*.

7102; Mon–Sat 10.30am–7pm; map p.137 C1
One of the best in town, with the latest novels.

Fact & Fiction
39 Basant Lok, opposite the Priya Cinema, Vasant Vihar; tel: 2614 6843; Wed–Mon 11am–8pm; map p.138 A3
Small but special, this bookshop has an excellent and select range of books.

Full Circle
23, 2nd floor, Middle Lane, Khan Market; tel: 2465 5641; Mon–Sat 9.30am–9.30pm; www.atfullcircle.com; metro: Khan Market; map p.137 D2
Good for art and design books; popular café upstairs.
SEE ALSO CAFÉS AND BARS, P.30

Theatre

Delhi has a strong tradition of theatre, and many performances take place nightly. Many are in Hindi, but you will find some productions of classic Western plays performed in English. A good source of information on the Delhi theatre scene is www.rangshala.com.

Traditional Dance Dramas and Theatre

Aside from its classical forms, India has many dance-dramas. These use

Andhra's tradition of male-only dance-drama, *kuchipudi*, is named after the village in the Krishna-Godvari delta in eastern India where it originated. The stories portrayed by the dancer are taken from the life of the Hindu god Krishna and his consort Bhama.

music and dance to tell a story, often one derived from Hindu epics. Although they come from all over the country, many are now performed on the concert stage and can often be seen in Delhi. One of the most spectacular performances you are likely to encounter is of *kathakali*. In this male Keralan dance form the characters – (from the *Ramayana* or *Mahabharata*) – put on large costumes and dramatic make-up to aid in the storytelling. The colours used in the make-up give the audience a clue as to the role of the character.

As well as these classical dramas (that also include *Manipuri* dance, and the Sanskrit theatre form *kutiyattam*, which is very close to the precepts laid down by Bharata in the *Natyasastra*), there are many local theatre forms. In the north one of

the more racy is the secular *nautanki*, unusual in that it only uses religious themes to denote concepts of good or evil and often draws on Muslim romance stories. In *nautanki* the actors use the drama to comment on current affairs, as they also do in the Tamil street theatre *terukkuttu*.

More religiously minded dramas performed at festivals are the *Ras* and *Ram lilas* of Braj and Varanasi that depict the lives of Krishna and Rama respectively, while both Kerala and Andhra Pradesh have shadow-puppet theatres akin to those found in Indonesia.
SEE ALSO MUSIC AND DANCE, P.94

Theatre Venues and Book Readings

The Attic
36 Regal Building, Connaught Place; tel: 2374 6050; www.the atticdelhi.org; metro: Rajiv Chowk; map p.137 C4

India Habitat Centre
Lodi Road; tel: 2468 2001; www.indiahabitat.org; map p.137 D1

India International Centre
40 Max Müller Marg; tel: 2461 9431; www.iicdelhi.nic.in; map p.137 D2

Kamani Auditorium
1 Copernicus Marg; tel: 4350 3351; www.kamaniauditorium. org; metro: Mandi House; map p.137 D4

Sangeet Natak Akademi
Rabindra Bhavan, Firoz Shah Road; tel: 2338 7246; www.sangeetnatak.com; metro: Mandi House; map p.137 D4

Triveni Kala Sangam
205 Tansen Marg; tel: 2371 8833; metro: Mandi House; map p.137 D4

Monuments

Delhi is littered with monuments, a tribute to its long history and waves of different rulers. Including two Unesco World Heritage Sites, they range from impressive tombs to tanks and demonstrations of the hubris and pomp of the British empire. The most important of those in the city are described below, but there is hardly a corner of Delhi that does not have a dome peeping out from among the crowded buildings, or a statue to an important national figure, saint or deity. Below are those monuments which are not places of worship; for those *see Religions and Religious Sites, p.104–111.*

Above: inside the Jantar Mantar.

Connaught Place

Jantar Mantar

Sansad Marg; www.delhi tourism.nic.in; daily sunrise–sunset; entrance charge; metro: Rajiv Chowk; map p.137 C4

A short distance south of Connaught Place on Sansad Marg lies the Jantar Mantar (derived from the Sanskrit, meaning 'instrument for calculation'). This fascinating collection of astrological instruments was built in 1724 by Maharaja Jai Singh of Jaipur, the first of a series of observatories he built in Jaipur, Ujjain, Mathura and Varanasi. He was driven to do

Visit Cornell University's www.jantarmantar.org for more information on Jantar Mantar. The website has some models of, and background information on, instruments and observatories in the collection.

this as the smaller brass astrolabes and quadrants he acquired were inaccurate, and so Jai Singh commissioned large-scale instruments made of brick and marble that would not move and would give more precise readings. The garden setting of this observatory is dominated by the cen

tral sundial, to the south of which lie instruments capable of ascertaining the position and altitude of the sun and the planets. On the right as you enter is a contraption which calculates the time in four of the world's time zones when Delhi time reaches noon.

Ugrasen ki Baoli

Off Hailey Road; daily sunrise–sunset; free; metro: Mandi House; map p.137 D4

This impressive *baoli*, or step-well (where steps led down to the varying water level to enable people to bathe and collect the water without the need for a rope and bucket) lies just off Hailey Road. It dates back to the 14th century and still appears as an impressive piece of engineering.

Old Delhi and Raj Ghat

Ajmeri Gate

Shraddhanand Marg, Old Delhi; daily sunrise–sunset; free; metro: New Delhi; map p.135 C2

The gates of the Old City were, in general, named after the main place that the road through them lead to. Ajmeri Gate was the one that pointed to Ajmer in

Left: the Dandi March statue on Willingdon Crescent, *see p.77*.

ascend to the throne. The British also used it as the execution place for the sons of Bahadur Shah, in revenge for the 1857 Uprising.

Raj Ghat
Mahatma Gandhi Marg; daily sunrise–sunset; free; metro: Pragati Maidan; map p.135 E2

To the south and east of the Lal Qila lie the cremation sites of some of Independent India's greatest leaders. Furthest to the south is a simple black-marble platform, known as Raj Ghat, where Mahatma Gandhi was cremated following his assassination in 1948. There are also two museums dedicated to 'Gandhiji' here.

To the north is Shanti Vana, 'Forest of Peace', the family cremation site for the Nehru-Gandhi dynasty; India's first prime minister, Jawaharlal Nehru, was cremated here in 1964, followed by his grandson Sanjay Gandhi in 1980, his daughter Indira Gandhi in 1984 and elder grandson, Rajiv, in 1991. To the north again is Vijay Ghat, 'Victory Ghat', where Nehru's successor, Prime Minister Lal Bahadur Shastri, was cremated. Kisan Ghat, to the south, is for Chaudhary Charan Singh, who was briefly prime minister in 1979. The

Rajasthan, site of an important Sufi shrine. This is one of the few that has survived in reasonable condition, and now sits in a small park.

Delhi Gate
Netaji Subhash Marg, Old Delhi; daily sunrise–sunset; free: metro: New Delhi; map p.135 D2

The well-preserved, south-facing Delhi Gate was so called because it gave access to the earlier cities of Delhi that lay to the south. Its red sandstone façade is in reasonable condition, and it is an unmistakable sight as you pass it on your way into Shahjahanabad.

Ghaziuddin Madrasa
Desh Bandhu Gupta Road, near Ajmeri Gate; daily sunrise–sunset; free; metro: New Delhi; map p.135 C2

Also known as the Anglo-Arabic School, this *Madrasa* (or school for religious instruction), now a little dilapidated, was established in 1692 by a minister at the court of the Mughal emperor Aurangzeb. The school, still

working, and attached mosque is an excellent example of mid- to late-Mughal architecture, and there have been plans put forward to renovate the building.

Khuni Darwaza
Bahadur Shah Zafar Marg; daily sunrise–sunset; free; metro: Pragati Maiden; map p.137 D4

This is thought to be the gateway to Shergarh, the 16th-century city of Sher Shah, who briefly overthrew the emperor Humayun. It has a bloodthirsty history: Aurangzeb displayed his elder brother's head here after he had been executed so that Aruangzeb could

Right: the Gandhi Memorial at Raj Ghat.

The Uprising of 1857 (known rather disparagingly by the British as the 'Mutiny') was said to have been triggered when a rumour spread that Indian *sepoys* (soldiers) were given cartridges to use that were covered in pork and cow fat: the first deeply offensive to the Muslims, the second to the the Hindus. Whatever the truth of this, it awoke considerable resentment among the Indians, and on 10 May 1857 the soldiers in Meerut mutinied. The movement gathered pace and, mustering around the elderly Mughal emperor Bahadur Shah, it soon turned into a full-blown war against the British. There was much misery and bloodshed on both sides, but eventually the better-armed British won. It was at this point that India was brought officially under the British crown and the Mughal emperor sent into exile in Burma. The unity between the Hindus and Muslims during the Uprising taught the British a lesson, and they not only imposed ever more draconian laws over the Indians (and excluded them from public office) but also put into place 'divide and rule' policies to ensure that such a unity would not threaten them again.

theme of death continues north along the river bank, with the Electric Crematorium and the Nigambodh Ghat Cremation Ground, where the Hindu population of Delhi conduct their funerals.
SEE ALSO MUSEUMS AND GALLERIES, P.85, 86; PARKS AND GARDENS, P.98; POLITICS, P.102

Turkman Gate
Turkman Bazaar Road, Old Delhi; daily sunrise–sunset; free; metro: New Delhi; map p.135 D2
One of the lesser-known gates of the old city walls still standing, Turkman Gate is in a crowded area, making it less easy to see than the others. Unlike Ajmeri and Delhi Gates, this one is named after a Muslim saint, Hazrat Shah Turkman Bayabani.

North Delhi

Coronation Memorial and The Durbar Site
Bhai Parmanand Marg, off the Outer Ring Road, Nirankari; daily sunrise–sunset; free; metro: Adarsh Nagar
Five km (3 miles) to the north of the Northern Ridge is the Coronation Memorial. This was the site of the three biggest durbar ceremonies under British rule, the first to pronounce Queen Victoria as

empress of India in 1877, followed by the 1903 celebration of Edward VII's accession to the throne and finally the 1911 coronation of George V. It was at the last that the foundation stones were laid for New Delhi. However, the site was found to be unsuitable and so the stones were quietly moved and built into the eastern walls of North and South Blocks.

The area's British connections meant that when Delhi's remaining British statues were rounded up during the 1960s, it was here that they were placed. The most impressive of these is the 1936 statue by Charles Jagger of George V at his coronation – the robe he wore for the occasion rippling behind him – which was originally located at India Gate. Also here are statues of Lords Irwin and Willingdon (both by Reid Dick) and one of Lord Chelmsford by the Indian sculptor M.S. Nagappa. The park surrounding the statues has recently been tidied up and it makes for an atmospheric excursion.

Flagstaff Tower
Magazine Road, Northern Ridge; daily sunrise–sunset; free; metro: Civil Lines
This British-built tower lies at

Left: the Mutiny Memorial and Durbar Ground.

the highest point of the ridge. It is famous as it is the point where the British – and other Europeans – gathered after the first attacks of the Uprising before moving on the Ambala and Meerut. The earliest British monument on the Ridge, it is not known for certain but it is thought that the tower was built as part of the military cantonment that was laid out by the British in 1828.

Kashmere Gate
Lothian Road, Old Delhi; daily sunrise–sunset; free; metro: Kashmere Gate; map p.135 D3
The northern entrance to Shahjahanabad was through this gate, the city's grandest and the only one to have two arches. It was from Kashmere Gate that the ruling family would leave to spend summer in the cool of Kashmir. The emperor Jahangir was famously enamoured of Kashmir, and he died en route in 1627. His son, Shah Jahan, also made several visits to Kashmir before he was deposed and imprisoned in Agra by his son Aurangzeb.

The gate was the scene of some of the heaviest fighting during the 1857 Uprising. After gathering on the Northern Ridge behind and breaching the walls with cannonball fire, British forces attacked Kashmere Gate on 14 September 1857, desperate to regain control of the city from the insurgents. Fighting continued for six days – evidence of cannonball fire can still be seen on the gate – until the British finally triumphed despite taking heavy losses.

The Mutiny Memorial
Rani Jhansi Road, Northern Ridge; daily sunrise–sunset; free; metro: Tis Hazari; map p.134 C3

At the southern end of the Northern Ridge is the large Neo-Gothic Mutiny Memorial (also known as the Ajit Garh, or 'Victory Tower'), built in 1862 to commemorate the British, and those Indians who fought with the British, who died in 1857. Panels on the memorial list the regiments of the Delhi Field Force, the dead officers and the numbers killed and wounded on the Ridge. From the memorial you get a view of how Delhi appeared to the attacking army.

Nicholson's Cemetery
Gokhale Marg, Old Delhi; daily sunrise–sunset; free; metro: Kashmere Gate; map p.135 D3
This small cemetery beside Kashmere Gate has a neo-Gothic entrance way but is chiefly important for the grave of John Nicholson who was regarded by the British as a hero for his actions during the recapture of Delhi during the 1857 Uprising.

Nigambodh Gate
Mahatma Gandhi Marg, Old Delhi; daily sunrise–sunset; free; metro: Kashmere Gate; map p.135 D3
One of the few remaining gateways into the Old City, it takes its name from the Nigambodh Ghat close by on the river. The ghat is sacred to Brahma, who is said to have bathed here.

Pir Ghalib
Ridge Road, Northern Ridge; daily sunrise–sunset; free; metro: Civil Lines; map p.134 C4
Just to the north of the Mutiny Memorial, in the grounds of the Hindu Rao Hospital, are the remains of what was either a hunting lodge or palace built by Feroz Shah Tughlaq during the 14th century. Known as the Pir Ghaib (the 'Disappearing Muslim Saint'), it is so called as a holy man is said to

have vanished while meditating on this spot. During the Uprising it was called the 'Observatory Tower' as it was used as a lookout. On the roof is a small hole which was used to drop a plumb line through during the Great Triangulation Survey of the 1830s, when the British made the first accurate mapping of India. Close by is one of Delhi's two Ashokan pillars (see box on p.79).

Roshanara Begum's Tomb
Roshanara Road; daily sunrise–sunset; free; metro: Pratap Nagar; map p.134 B4
This sits in Roshanara Bagh, laid out by Shah Jahan's youngest daughter. At the centre of the park is her tomb, the site for which she set out herself in 1650 and where she was buried in 1671. The low building with *chatris* (open pavilions) at each corner is simple but attractive.
SEE ALSO PARKS AND GARDENS, P.99

Rajpath and Chanakyapuri

Dandi March Statue
Willingdon Crescent; daily sunrise–sunset; free; metro: Central Secretariat; map p.136 B3
This impressive bronze by the

Right: India Gate, *see p.78.*

77

Indian sculptor Devi Prasad Roy shows Gandhi leading the demonstrators on his march to Dandi on the Gujarat coast to protest against the British imposing a salt tax.

India Gate
Rajpath; daily sunrise–sunset; free; metro: Central Secretariat; map p.137 D3

India Gate, a 42-m (138-ft) high archway, was built by Lutyens at the eastern end in 1931 to honour Indian soldiers who died during World War I and on the Northwest Frontier (their names are carved onto the walls of the arch). There is now an 'eternal flame' commemorating those killed in the 1971 war with Pakistan. It is particularly impressive when lit up at night. Close by is the empty canopy that used to contain the monumental sculpture of George V now at the Durbar Site in North Delhi *(see p.76)*.

Lodi Gardens and Nizamuddin

Atgah Khan's Tomb
Nizamuddin West; daily sunrise–sunset; free; metro: Jangpura; map p.137 E1

Part of the *dargah* complex at Nizamuddin, this is the tomb of one of the courtiers of the emperor Akhbar. Atgah Khan was killed by Adham Khan, whose mother built the Khairul Manazil Masjid. Although the tomb, built in 1566–7, is small, it is a splendid example of Mughal architecture, with much of its original decoration still intact.

Chaunsath Khamba
Nizamuddin West, by the Ghalib Library; daily sunrise–sunset; free; metro: Jangpura; map p.137 E2

This is another site near the Nizamuddin *dargah*. The marble tomb is that of Atgah Khan's son, Mirza Aziz Kokaltash. The delicate structure was built in 1624–4 and has 64 pillars (*chaunsath* in Urdu) that support its roof.

Humayun's Tomb
Mathura Road; www.asi.nic.in; daily sunrise–sunset; entrance charge; metro: JLN Stadium; map p.137 E2

At the eastern end of Lodi Road is Humayun's Tomb. Set in beautiful gardens, this red sandstone monument is the

finest Mughal building in Delhi (listed as a Unesco World Heritage Site in 1993) and the prototype for the Taj Mahal. It was commissioned by Humayun's senior widow, Bega Begum, who camped on site throughout the nine-year project, which was completed in 1565.

The beneficiary of a sensitive restoration project in 2003, the tomb is one of the best-preserved Moghul monuments in India. The complex is actually home to a large number of tombs, including those of many royal family members and even Humayun's barber.

On entering the complex, you'll notice a stone gateway leading through the wall on the right. Through this lies **Isa Khan's Tomb**, which, though unrestored, has an evocative atmosphere. Parts of the original tilework remain, giving an insight into how the building must have originally looked.

Coming back through the gateway, turn right and the second archway will lead you into the formal gardens surrounding the main tomb. These are laid out in the traditional *charbagh* design, divided by water channels into 32 separate areas – those at the Taj Mahal follow the same pattern. The three high walls that enclose the garden are testimony to the changing course of the Yamuna River, which originally ran directly past the tomb and would have formed the fourth boundary.

The main tomb building sits on a red sandstone platform; the small arches lining the platform lead to the tombs of lesser royals. The building itself, also of red sandstone, is inlaid with black-and-white marble and

Left: the Bara Gumbad in Lodi Gardens.

Above: the beautiful symmetry of Humayun's Tomb.

has at its centre the octagonal chamber containing the tomb of Humayun himself, as well as other Mughal nobles. The tomb was a witness to the last stand of Bahadur Shah and his sons, where they had hidden during the 1857 Uprising. The 38-m (125-ft) high dome was the first of its type in India; domes had until then been simple hemispheres rather than the fuller onion shape seen here.

Khan-i-Khanan's Tomb
Mathura Road, Nizamuddin East; www.asi.nic.in; daily sunrise–sunset; entrance charge; metro: Jangpura; map p.137 E1

To the south of Humayun's Tomb lies the tomb of Abdur Rahim Khan, son of Akhbar's most loyal protector in his early years, who carried the title of Khan-i-Khanan. He was later remembered chiefly for his poetry, which is still popular in India today. His tomb was designed along the lines of Humayun's, and originally had a marble dome, but this was taken off to be used on Safdarjang's Tomb. Somehow the building

seems more impressive for its distressed façade, and, as this is not as often visited as some of the other Mughal sites, the tomb itself is quietly atmospheric.

LODI GARDENS TOMBS AND MOSQUE
Lodi Road; daily sunrise–sunset; free; metro: Jor Bagh; map p.137 C/D2

There are five important monuments hidden away within Lodi Gardens.

> Delhi has two of the pillars originally set up by the Mauryan emperor Ashoka in the 3rd century BC, throughout his empire, inscribed with the Buddha's edicts. They were both brought to Delhi by the sultan Feroz Shah Tughlaq during the 14th century; one was erected on the Northern Ridge near the Pir Ghaib, the other in Firoz Shah Kotla *(see also Forts, p.54)*. The better-preserved of the two pillars is the one in Firoz Shah Kotla, and the Brahmi inscription can be clearly seen on the 12.8-m (42-ft) polished sandstone column.

Arthpula
This small bridge close to the tomb of Sikander Lodi dates back to Mughal times (probably the late 16th century) and has eight supports (from which it gets its name; *arth* is HIndi for 'eight').

The Bara Gumbad and Mosque
This tomb, and its adjacent mosque, is known as the Great Dome (from the Hindi *bara*, 'large', and *gumbad*, 'dome'). It was built for an unknown Lodi noble and it prefigures many of the architectural developments of the Mughals. The mosque is made of ashlar stone and is decorated with inscriptions from the Qur'an.

The Shish Gumbad
The 'glazed dome' – decorated with blue tiles – also dates from the Lodi period. Again, it is not certain who was buried here, but architecturally it resembles the Bara Gumbad.

Muhammad Shah's Tomb
The octagonal tomb of the Sayyid ruler Muhammad Shah (1434–44) is close to Lodi

79

Above: the *madrasa* and tomb at Hauz Khas.

Road. As well as the ruler himself it also contains the graves of a number of his relatives.

Sikander Lodi's Tomb

This tomb, similar in many respects to that of Muhammad Shah although better-preserved, is in the north of the gardens by an ornamental lake (part of which the Arthpula spans). It is of later design, built in 1517, and retains its outer walls.

Najaf Khan's Tomb

Aurobindo Marg, Lodi Colony; daily sunrise–sunset; free; metro: Jor Bagh; map p.137 C1

The low, plain tomb of the Persian nobleman Najaf Khan lies near the Safdarjang Flyover. The surrounding walls must originally have been impressive but are now quite ruined. The grounds have been tidied up and the rather sprawling building, built in 1782, is strangely attractive.

Nila Gumbad

Harsha Road; daily sunrise–sunset; free; metro: JLN Stadium; map p.137 E2

The blue-tiled dome of this tomb can be seen from the eastern end of the enclosure of Humayun's Tomb. It is thought to have been built in 1626 for Fahim Khan, an attendant at the court of the

> The name of the octagonal tomb Sabz Burj means 'green tower', although during its restoration by the Archaeological Survey of India, the 'green' tiles were discovered to be vivid blue.

Mughal emperor Jahangir.

Sabz Burj

Mathura Road; daily sunrise–sunset; free; metro: JLN Stadium; map p.137 E2

Set in the middle of a roundabout where Lodi Road meets Mathura Road is this octagonal tomb with a double dome covered with tiles. It dates from the early Mughal period and is the only tomb in Delhi built in a typical Central Asian style.

Safdarjang's Tomb

Aurobindo Marg; www.asi.nic.in; daily sunrise–sunset; entrance charge; metro: Race Course; map p.136 C1

Safdarjung's Tomb and its adjoining rose garden are at the western end of Lodi Road just across Aurobindo Marg. This huge monument, dating from 1753, is the last significant piece of Mughal architecture to be built in Delhi. The gardens, like those at Humayun's Tomb,

have been renovated and are now beautifully maintained. Safdarjang was *vazir* (chief minister) under the Mughal emperor Muhammad Shah. It is patterned after Humayun's Tomb, but its proportions are not quite as elegant as those of the earlier building. However, it has some wonderful decoration, and the corner towers of the tomb itself are delightfully ornate.

South Delhi

Chor Minar

Panchsheel Crossing, Hauz Khas Enclave; daily sunrise–sunset; free; metro: Hauz Khas; map p.138 C2

The 'thieves' tower' dates back to the Khilji period and sits in an attractive garden. However, its purpose seems to have been a gruesome one; it is said that the severed heads of criminals were displayed in the niches that line the tower as a deterrent to others who might be feeling a bit light-fingered.

Firoz Shah Tughlaq's *Madrasa* and Tomb

Hauz Khas Village; daily sunrise–sunset; free; metro: Hauz Khas; map p.138 B3

These can be found at surviving remains of Delhi's second city at Hauz Khas (the 'royal tank'). The area takes its name from the reservoir created by Ala-ud-din Khilji in around 1300 to provide water for his new city. Half a century later Firoz Shah Tughlaq repaired the tank and founded a *madrasa* (school) by the side of the reservoir, as well as creating an enclosure for his own tomb. The classrooms are arranged in an L-shape around the tank, while the tomb itself has a pretty marble-and-sandstone façade and an attractive stone railing.

Mehrauli and Tughlaqabad

Bhulbhulaiyan

Mehrauli Archaeological Park, Mehrauli Village; daily sunrise–sunset; free; metro: Qutab Minar; map p.138 B1

This huge octagonal building is on the right as soon as you enter Mehrauli Village. It is the tomb of Adham Khan, a general in the 16th-century Mughal army. Ironically, the tomb was erected by the emperor Akhbar who had Adham Khan put to death. The tomb is built on the walls of Lalkot, the city of the Tomara Rajputs.

Ghiyasuddin's Tomb

Mehrauli–Dadarpur Road, Tughlaqabad; daily sunrise–sunset; free; metro: Tughlaqabad

The 14th-century tomb of this Tughlaq ruler originally sat on an island on a lake that lay to the south of Tughlaqabad fort. It is noted for its sloping walls, with alternating red sandstone and marble, and for its fortified appearance.

SEE ALSO FORTS, P.57

Hauz-i-Shamsi and Jahaz Mahal

Mehrauli Village; daily sunrise–sunset; free; metro: Qutab Minar

At the southern end of Mehrauli Village is the Huaz-i-Shamsi, a large tank built by Iltutmish in 1230 into which a spring runs. The pavilion on the banks of the tank, the Jahaz Mahal ('ship palace') dates from the Lodi period.

Jamali Kamali

Mehrauli Archaeological Park, Mehrauli Village; daily sunrise–sunset; free; metro: Qutab Minar; map p.138 B1

This beautifully decorated small tomb is located just to the east of Mehrauli Village. To the right of the tomb is a mosque dating from the 16th century which was built by the Sufi poet Sheikh Fazlullah, whose pen-name was Jamali and who is buried in the tomb. The identity of Kamali, who is also buried here, remains a mystery.

Lal Gumbad

Sadhana Enclave, Panchshila Park South; daily sunrise–sunset; free; metro: Hauz Khas; map p.139 C2

This small tomb is thought to be the burial place of the saint Kabir-ud-din Auliya. Erected in the mid-14th century, the round dome supported on 12 square pillars is one of the most important pre-Mughal monuments in the city.

Right: the Quwwat-ul-Islam, iron pillar and Qutb Minar, *see p.82–3.*

81

THE QUTB MINAR COMPLEX

Qutb Minar, off the Mehrauli–Gurgaon Road; www.asi.nic.in; daily sunrise–sunset; entrance charge; metro: Qutab Minar; map p.138 B1

Made a Unesco World Heritage Site in 1993, the Qutb Minar and the buildings which surround this tower mark the centre of the first of the Delhi Sultanates. It was the first major Islamic construction in India.

The Qutb Minar

The Qutb Minar itself was built by Qutb-ud-din Aibak, the Turkish general appointed governor of Delhi by Muhammad bin Sam; he later reigned as sultan. Its construction followed the near obliteration by Muhammad's troops of all religious monuments on the North Indian plain, be they Hindu, Buddhist or Jain, and

> The iron pillar at the Qutb Minar is made from an exceptionally pure alloy that does not rust. The inscriptions on the pillar date it to the 4th century BC, it continues to puzzle metallurgists, who cannot explain how it was made.

was intended to celebrate the victory of Islam. Qutb-ud-din started work in 1199, and completed three storeys before his death in 1210. His son-in-law, Iltutmish, succeeded him and added a fourth storey.

After twice sustaining lightning damage during the 1300s, the tower was renovated by Firoz Shah Tughlaq, who also added a fifth storey topped by an ornate cupola. An earthquake in 1803 forcibly removed the cupola, however, and it was replaced

in 1829 by another built by Major Robert Smith. Not quite as elegant as the original, the British engineer's handiwork was removed in 1848 and now lies in the adjacent gardens. The tower today stands 73 m (239 ft) high, tapering in diameter from 14 m (46 ft) at the base to just 2.5 m (8 ft) at the top.

Quwwat-ul-Islam

Next to the tower stands India's first mosque, Quwwat-ul-Islam (the 'Might of Islam') Masjid. Started by Qutb-ud-din in 1192, the original mosque was built from the remains of 27 Hindu and Jain temples, a fact evinced by the panoply of styles within. Of particular note is the sandstone screen which forms the mosque's façade, originally Indo-Islamic in style but with more purely Islamic later additions. Iltutmish extended

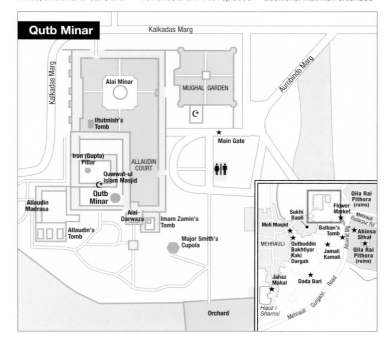

the mosque, incorporating as he did so the Qutb Minar within the boundary walls, and thus producing the first example of a mosque with integral minaret.

Iltutmish's Tomb

Iltutmish's Tomb lies to the west of the mosque, the earliest surviving example of an Indian ruler's tomb. The quality of the interior carving is particularly fine. The tomb is thought to have originally been covered by a dome which has since collapsed, fragments of which can be seen lying around the building.

The Alai Darwaza and Alai Minar

These two later additions to the complex were made by Alu-ad-din Khilji in the early 14th century. The first is a domed monumental gateway that leads to the Quwwat-ul-Islam. The second is the unfinished remains of a huge minaret that was to have been taller than the Qutb Minar.

Satpula

Press Enclave Marg, near the Khirki Masjid; daily sunrise–sunset; free; metro: Malviya Nagar; map p.139 D2

This extrordinary structure was part of the city walls of the Tughlaq city of Jahanapanah. It was designed to regulate, and hold back, the flow of water of the small river that ran through the city. There are seven (as in the Hindi 'sat') openings that acted as sluice gates.

Sultan Ghari's Tomb

Off Mahipalpur–Mehrauli Road, Vasant Kunj; www.asi.nic.in; daily sunrise–sunset; entrance charge; metro: Chhatarpur

One of the least visited and most interesting monuments in Delhi, the tomb of Iltutmish's son, Nasir-ud-din, displays an interesting mix of Islamic and Hindu styles and

Above: inside the Jamali Kamali and restoration in Mehrauli, *see p.81*.

has an ornately decorated *mihrab* (prayer niche) on its western wall. The structure has a quiet austerity, with its domed bastions of sandstone, its colonnaded enclosure and octagonal tomb-chamber.

Surajkund

Surajkund Village, Haryana; daily sunrise–sunset; free; metro: Badarpur

Just over the Delhi-Haryana border is this tank built on the site of Surajpal, the city of the Tomar Rajputs. The tank is believed to date back to at least the 11th century, and its name is said to derive from Surya, the sun god, to whom it is thought there was once a temple on the site. The embankments are stepped

to enable people to reach the water as the level drops during the summer.

Vijay Mandal

Vijay Mandal Enclave, Sarvapriya Vihar; daily sunrise–sunset; free; metro: Badarpur

This is the ruined remains of the palace of Muhammad bin Tughlaq, the seat of power of the city of Jahanpanah. It was memorably described by the Arab adventurer Ibn Batuta who travelled in India during the first half of the 14th century; at the time it was apparently a splendid sight, hung with silks and replete with martial pomp. It is possible to climb up through the rooms to the octgonal structure on the flat roof. From here there is a wonderful view across the city.

83

Museums and Galleries

The collections in Delhi's museums and art galleries range from superbly displayed artefacts from everyday life, to the luxury coaches of a maharaja's train, to a recreation of Louis XIV's toilet. As the capital of the country it is fitting that some of the finest collections of Indian art should be here; the national museums of archaeology and modern art have superb holdings and are well worth a visit, while the story of modern India is told through a series of museums dedicated to the country's leaders since Independence.

Above: multiple Gandhis crop up on postage stamps.

Entrance fees can vary quite widely in Delhi. For most of the major institutions (such as the National Museum or National Gallery of Modern Art) foreign visitors are charged a higher rate than locals. The fee is usually between Rs 250 and Rs 500. For some places, however, no such distinction is in place and the fee can be very low, often around Rs 2–10.

Connaught Place

Lalit Kala Akademi

Rabindra Bhavan, Firoz Shah Road; tel: 2338 7241; Mon–Sat 11am– 6pm; entrance charge; metro: Mandi House; map p.137 D4

This is the headquarters of the national institution for the visual arts. Temporary exhibitions are held in the Lalit Kala Akademi's gelleries of modern and contemporary Indian art. They also hold an international Triennale, the most recent being in 2008.

National Museum of Natural History

FICCI Museum Building, Barakhamba Road; tel: 2331 4849; www.nmnh.nic.in; Tue–Sun 10am–5pm; entrance charge; metro: Mandi House; map p.137 D4

Better-displayed than some natural history museums in India, but the National Museum of Natural History is still a bit like a trip to the past. As with most other museums that now trumpet their commitment to environmental protection, many of the exhibits are the legacy of the bloodthirsty mass slaughter of large mammals and the ghoulish preoccupation with pickling hapless reptiles that seemed to count as scientific investigation

during colonial times. Set out over four floors, the museum guides you from the classification of life, via ecology and conservation, to an investigation of DNA and the basic building blocks of life.

National Philatelic Museum

Dak Bhavan, Sardar Patel Chowk, Sansad Marg; tel: 2303 6447; Mon–Fri 10am–5pm; entrance charge; metro: Patel Chowk; map p.136 C3

Perhaps of minority interest, but the national collection of philately has a number of rare stamps and first-day covers from around the world. There is also a small shop where you can buy stamps.

Left: visitors wander through the National Museum, *see p.88*.

cinating objects that give a good impression of the immense diversity of India's musical traditions. Some of the most interesting exhibits are those of the Adivasi instruments from Central and Northeast India, which include a great variety of drums, trumpets and rattles.

Old Delhi and Raj Ghat

Archaeological Museum

Mumtaz Mahal, Lal Qila; tel: 2326 7961; www.asi.nic.in; Sat–Thur 9am–5pm; entrance charge; metro: Chandni Chowk; map p.135 D3

The museum at the Lal Qila *(see p.55)* has a fine display of Mughal-era artefacts, many connected with the history of the fort itself. It is particularly noted for its collections of miniature paintings and calligraphy, although there are also some good examples of Mughal textiles.

Gandhi Darshan

Raj Ghat; tel: 2339 2710; www.gandhismriti.nic.in; Tue–Sun 10am–5pm; free; metro: Pragati Maidan; map p.135 E1–2

This small museum at Raj Ghat has a good collection of paintings and photos of Gandhi and his life, as well as charting the history of his revolutionary Satyagraha

Shankar's International Dolls Museum

Nehru House, 4 Bahadur Shah Zafar Marg; tel: 2331 6970; www.childrensbooktrust.com; Tue–Sun 10am–6pm; entrance charge; metro: Pragati Maidan; map p.135 D1

A huge collection of dolls. In sometimes fanciful national and regional dress, they represent all the different parts of India as well as most of the countries in the world.

Srinivas Mallah Theatre Crafts Museum

5 Deen Dayal Upadhyay Marg, near Government Girls Higher Secondary School; tel: 2331 2972; Tue–Sat 10am–5pm; entrance charge; metro: Barakhamba Road; map p.135 D1

India has a myriad of local theatre traditions, and this small museum collects and preserves items associated with these dying art forms. As well as costumes, there are some fascinating masks and puppets (look out for the large shadow puppets from Andhra Pradesh) on display.

Vadya Darsan

Sangeet Natak Akademi, Rabindra Bhavan, Firoz Shah Road; tel: 2338 7246; www.sangeetnatak.org; Mon–Fri 9.30am–6pm; entrance charge; metro: Mandi House; map p.137 D4

In the same fashion as the Lalit Kala Akademi *(left)* the Sangeet Natak Akademi is the Indian government's national institution for the study and preservation of music and dance. In Rabindra Bhavan is their small museum of musical instruments (its name literally means 'seeing instruments'). Little-visited, it has some fas-

Right: Gandhi's words are still inspirational.

(non-violence) movement that confounded the British.

Gandhi Smarak Sangrahalaya

Raj Ghat; tel: 2339 2709; www.gandhismriti.nic.in; Fri–Wed 9.30am–5.30pm; free; metro: Pragati Maidan; map p.135 E1–2

The second of the two museums dedicated to the 'Mahatma' ('Great Soul' as Gandhi was dubbed) at Raj Ghat. This one houses a display of Gandhi's admirably small and austere number of personal belongings and also has a library of recordings of his speeches. A film about his life is shown on Sundays.

SEE ALSO POLITICS, P.102

Indian War Memorial Museum

Naubat Khana, Lal Qila; tel: 2327 3703; www.asi.nic.in; Sat–Thur 10am–5pm; entrance charge; metro: Chandni Chowk; map p.135 D3

This small collection of arms mostly comes from World War I, with few traditional weapons. It is worth a look for the diorama of the battle of Panipat (1526) between the Mughal emperor Babur and Ibrahim Lodi.

National Children's Museum

Bal Bhavan, 1 Kotla Marg; tel: 2323 2672; www.national balbhavan.nic.in; Tue–Sat 9am–5.30pm; entrance charge; metro: Barakhamba Road; map p.135 D1

Part of the national institution to promote children and children's rights, this museum has child-friendly galleries which give a (not entirely unbiased) description of Indian history and culture.

Swatantrata Sangram Sangrahalaya

Old Barracks Building, Lal Qila; tel: 2326 2238; www.asi.nic.in; entrance charge; Sat–Thur 10am–5pm; metro: Chandni Chowk; map p.135 D3

When the army began to vacate the Lal Qila during the 1990s, one of the old buildings was turned into this museum outlining the history of the Indian Independence Movement, from the Uprising of 1857 to freedom from the British in 1947. Although some of the exhibits seem a bit lacklustre, it does give a very thorough overview of this critical period of Indian history.

Right: newspaper reports and the glass walkway at the Indira Gandhi Memorial Museum.

Swatantrata Senani Museum

Salimgarh, Lal Qila; tel: 2326 7961; www.asi.nic.in; entrance charge; Sat–Thur 10am–5pm; metro: Chandni Chowk; map p.135 D3

Set in an old army building just inside Salimgarh fort, this has a small exhibition dedicated to the Indian National Army, set up by the freedom fighter Subhash Chandra Bose to fight the British during World War II.

North Delhi

Azad Hindi Gram

NH10, Tikri Kalan, near the Haryana Border; tel: 2835 3102; www.delhitourism.nic.in; daily 10am–6pm; entrance charge; metro: Badli

Now very run-down, this complex of domed buildings was devised as a museum commemorating the Bengali freedom fighter Subhash Chandra Bose. Unfortunately the grandiose patriotic message is rather let down by its current state, and you would

be quite justified in avoiding making the trip out here unless you had a very good reason to be in the area.

Rajpath and Chanakyapuri

Archaeological Museum

Purana Qila; tel: 2435 5387; www.asi.nic.in; Sat–Thur 10am–5pm; entrance charge; metro: Pragati Maidan; map p.137 E3

Run by the Archaeological Survey of India, the museum is more informative than some others in the city. It concentrates on finds made at Purana Qila (mostly dating from a large excavation in 1969) and it illustrates the site's long occupation. Among the finds are a toy ram from the Mauryan period, terracottas from the time of the Rajputs and some beautiful glazed pots of the Delhi Sultanate.

Crafts Museum

Pragati Maidan, Bhairon Road; tel: 2337 1641; www.national craftsmuseum.nic.in; Tue–Sun July– Sept 9.30am–5pm, Oct– June 9.30am–6pm; entrance charge; metro: Pragati Maidan; map p.137 E3

This is one of the capital's finest museums, giving an excellent overview of the country's myriad craft traditions. The grounds contain a series of huts built in a wide variety of regional styles (look for those from the northeast built on stilts) and many of the walls are decorated by paintings by Adivasi artists from Central India. There are often demonstrations by regional craftsmen and a good crafts shop. The fascinating exhibition galleries have displays of Adivasi art, wood-carving and textiles. There are bhuta figures from Karnataka, brightly decorated Naga objects from the northeast and some wonderful bronzes from Orissa. The textile galleries are superb – the collections run to over 22,000 objects – as well as some astounding (especially

> If you are intending to buy some of the many excellent Indian crafts and textiles while you are in the country it might be worth taking a couple of trips to the museums in Delhi that give an excellent overview of what might be on offer. It will also give you a good guide to the quality you might expect. Be warned though, really good pieces will not come cheap.

the Kashmere) examples of embroidery. There are also weaving demonstrations.

Gandhi Smriti

5 Tees January Marg; tel: 2301 2843; www.gandhismriti.nic.in; Tue–Sun 9.30am–5.30pm; entrance charge; metro: Udyog Bhavan; map p.137 C2

Also known as the **Birla House**, the Gandhi Smriti is a museum and memorial set in the residence of the industrialist G.D. Birla. Gandhi was staying here on 30 January 1948 when he was approached by a young man, Nathuram Vinayak Godse, a right-wing Hindu in the RSS who assassinated him for what was perceived as Gandhi's pro-Muslim stance. In the garden the place where he was shot is marked by a simple memorial. The route taken by the assassinated leader is marked out, this time by a series of concrete 'footsteps'. The building also has photographs of Gandhi and a few of his possessions.

Indira Gandhi Memorial Museum

1 Safdarjang Road; tel: 2301 0094; Tue–Sun 9.30am–5pm; free; metro: Udyog Bhavan; map p.136 C2

Commemorated at this museum is another political

Left: a craft demonstration and exhibits at the Crafts Museum.

While in the past Delhi's museums have had a certain run-down charm (often hiding truly wonderful exhibits), many are now undergoing a make-over, prompted in part by exemplary displays by institutions such as the Sanskriti Foundation. However, don't expect lots of glittering glass and state-of-the-art facilities everywhere; these changes will take time.

life and assassination. The bungalow here was Indira Gandhi's residence and the place where she was killed by her Sikh bodyguards in retaliation for her order to attack the Golden Temple in Amritsar, the Sikhs' holiest shrine. Blood stains are still visible at the spot in the gardens. Inside you can see her study and her wedding *sari*, woven by Nehru. The path of her last moments is marked by a glass walkway in the garden.

SEE ALSO POLITICS, P.102

Jawaharlal Nehru Memorial Museum

Teen Murti Bhavan, Teen Murti Marg; tel: 2301 5268; www.neh rumemorial.com; Tue–Sun 10am–3pm; free; metro: Udyog Bhavan; map p.136 B2

Teen Murti Bhavan houses the Jawaharlal Nehru Memorial Museum in the prime minister's former residence. Nehru's study, sitting room and bedroom have been preserved, and there is a very detailed exhibition explaining the history of the Independence struggle. The modesty of the interiors reflects well on one of India's greatest leaders. The research library here is one of the most important for modern Indian political history. In the

grounds is the **Nehru Planetarium**, and behind the mansion are beautifully maintained gardens.

SEE ALSO CHILDREN, P.35

National Gallery of Modern Art

Jaipur House, India Gate; tel: 2338 4640; www.ngmaindia. gov.in; Tue–Sun 10am–5pm; entrance charge; metro: Central Secretariat; map p.137 D3

The nation's premier collection of contemporary and modern Indian painting and sculpture is housed in this Lutyens-era domed building just off Rajpath. Initially intended as the Delhi residence of the Maharaja of Jaipur, in 1954 (after the abolition of the 'Princely States' at Independence) it was turned into an art gallery. The first floor houses the permanent collection, with excellent examples of the

Right: the National Gallery of Modern Art.

Right: the house and study at Teen Murti Bhavan.

work of luminaries such as M.F. Hussain and Jamini Roy. The ground floor is given over to major exhibitions and retrospectives of contemporary Indian artists, including photographers.

National Museum

Janpath; tel: 2301 9272; www.nationalmuseumindia. gov.in; Tue–Sun 10am–5pm; entrance charge; metro: Central Secretariat; map p.137 C3

The country's main national collection is noted for its Indian sculpture and jewellery collections, Chola bronzes and a Buddhist gallery, including a carved Buddhist gateway from Sanchi. The ground floor has prehistoric items found during excavations on the Subcontinent;

among the most important artefacts here are those from the Harappan city at Mohenjadaro (including the famous small bronze statue of a dancing girl). Also on the ground floor are some fabulous Gupta terracottas, including a bust of Vishnu from a temple near Lal Kot, Delhi's first city. Look out as well for the South India sculpture (where there is a splendid Chola bronze of Siva Nataraja) and the excellent collection of Buddhist bronzes. The jewellery collections – held in a well-fortified safe room – have some impressive examples of Mughal bling as well as some much earlier examples of Indian gold work.

On the first floor is the outstanding collection of Mughal manuscripts and miniatures, as well as Central Asian antiquities discovered by the British archaeologist Aurel Stein. Especially good on the second floor is the Verrier Elwin collection of Adivasi art, acquired by the great anthropologist and campaigner for Adivasi rights, from the northeastern, central and southern Indian states.

National Rail Museum
Chanakyapuri; tel: 2688 1816; www.nrm.indianrailways.gov.in;

Tue–Sun Oct–Mar 9.30am–1pm, 1.30–5.30pm, Apr–Sept 9.30am–1pm, 1.30–7.30pm; entrance charge; metro: Race Course; map p.136 B1

The National Rail Museum lies just off Shanti Path in Chanakyapuri, and is well worth a visit. There are some interesting period coaches and a large array of steam engines, including the huge *Garratt*, built in 1930 in Manchester. In contrast to the somewhat basic accommodation that tends to predominate on India's railways, have a look at the luxury coaches previously used by the country's maharajas. As well as the informative indoor displays outlining the functioning of the modern Indian rail network (including locomotive design, signalling and trackwork), there is also an unusual working steam monorail that takes visitors around the site.

National Science Centre Museum
Near Gate 1, Pragati Maidan, Bhairon Road; tel: 2337 1297; www.nscdelhi.org; daily 10am–5.30pm; entrance charge; metro: Pragati Maidan; map p.137 E3

Better than it at first sounds, this museum, set up in 1992, should appeal to children and adults alike with its clear dis-

plays outlining the basics of biology, physics and engineering. There are lots of buttons to press and handles to turn, as well as cases of impressive-looking scientific instruments.

Lodi Gardens and Nizamuddin

Ghalib Academy
Basti Hazrat Nizamuddin West; tel: 2435 1098; www.ghalib academy.org; Mon–Sat 11am–6pm; metro: Jangpura; map p.137 E2

This little-known museum and library is dedicated to the famous Urdu poet Mirza Asad Ullah Khan Ghalib (1797–1869). Regarded as one of the greatest figures in Indian literature, his exquisite verse is sensuous and provides a vivid glimpse of the Muslim high culture of 19th-century Delhi. The small museum has a collection of fine paintings inspired by the poems, including works by M.F. Hussain, Satiate Jugular and Anise Farooqui. The library has over 10,000 volumes, and the academy has an active publishing programme as well as holding lectures and events.

National Police Museum
Block 4, CGO Complex, Lodi

89

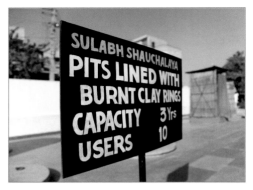

Road; tel: 2436 1812; Mon–Fri 10am–5pm; free; metro: JLN Stadium; map p.137 D1

This museum deals with the more salubrious side of the Indian Police, the part actually to do with solving crimes and arresting miscreants rather than the 'They fell downstairs' or the 'Give me Rs 10,000' bits. Among the more interesting exhibits are the arrest warrant for Bhagat Singh who was executed by the British for revolutionary activity, and a shotgun given to the police by Nehru. As you might imagine, tales of gruesome murders abound (and not all of them were committed by the police themselves).

Tibet House Museum
1 Institutional Area, Lodi Road; tel: 2461 1515; www.tibethouse newdelhi.org; Mon–Fri 9.30am–5.30pm; entrance charge; metro: JLN Stadium; map p.137 D1

Tibet House was founded by the Dalai Lama in 1965. Although only tiny, this museum of Tibetan art and culture has some exceptionally fine exhibits. The scroll paintings and *thankas* are exquisite, and there are also interesting sculptures and Tibetan musical instruments on display. There is a small shop attached to the museum, mostly selling books and catalogues, as well as a research library.

Left: the Sulabh International Museum of Toilets.

South Delhi

Air Force Museum
Palam Airport; tel: 2568 7194; www.armedforces.nic.in/airforce; Wed–Sun 10am–5pm; free; metro: Airport

Although quite a way out of town (near the commerical domestic airport), this museum is worth a visit if you are staying out this way or have some time to kill between flights. There are currently plans afoot to expand and modernise the museum, but at present there are a number of military aircraft that between them tell the history of the India Air Force (including one plane damaged during the 1971 war with Pakistan) as well as mock-ups of Soviet and US spaceships.

Sulabh International Museum of Toilets
Sulabh Bhawan, Mahavir Enclave, Palam Dabri Marg; tel: 2503 1518; www.sulabh toiletmuseum.org; Mon–Sat 10am–5pm; free; metro: Uttam Nagar East

Set up by the social campaigner Dr Bindeshwar Pathak, this museum traces the evolution of sanitation from its earliest beginnings, via the chamber pot (the Viennese ceramics are lovely), to the most modern flush systems (the mock-up of Louis XIV's bog is quite something). As well as its educational value, the more serious side to the museum and the attached organisation is Dr Pathak's work in campaigning for better sanitation across India, and for better treatment of India's sanitation workers, who come from the very lowest strata of the caste system and who still face considerable discrimination.

Zakir Hussain Memorial

Jamia Millia Islamia University, Okhla; tel: 2698 1717; Sat–Thur 10am–4.30pm; free; metro: Okhla

Although this is probably one for specialists, Dr Zakir Hussain was a great scholar and President of India 1967–9. He helped found Jamia Milia Islamia University, where the museum is located, as well as the university at Aligarh. The museum contains photographs of his life and also a substantial archive of his papers.

Mehrauli and Tughlakabad

Sanskriti Foundation

C11, Qutb Institutional Area, Mehrauli; tel: 2696 3226; www.sanskritifoundation.org; Tue–Sun 10am–5pm; free; metro: Malviya Nagar; map p.138 B2

The museums below are part of the Sanskriti Foundation, a non-profit organisation which aims to nurture artistic talent and thus help to preserve India's cultural heritage. This complex, known as 'Kendra', houses artists' residences, workshops, studios and galleries in addition to the two museums. The curators are keen for museum visitors to interact with the resident artists, often a fascinating experience for both parties. There are plans to open a separate Museum of Textiles to show off the foundation's substantial collection of Indian fabrics.

Museum of Everyday Art

This is one of the most fascinating and best-displayed museums in Delhi. The exhibits take in all manner of traditional artefacts and are laid out according to a life cycle, from the toys of children, to writing tools for students, to household objects for a family, including pots, pans and *puja* paraphernalia.

Museum of Indian Terracotta

Still a living tradition in India, the use to which terracotta has been put on the Subcontinent ranges from everyday pots for water and cooking to sculptures. The most famous of the latter are the large terracotta horses made in Tamil Nadu as cult objects used in the worship of the god Ayyanar. The pieces are beautifully displayed in a series of open galleries, some decorated with traditional wall-painting.

There is a thriving art scene in Delhi, and the following commercial galleries are all well established:

Delhi Art Gallery (11 Hauz Khas Village; tel: 4600 5300; www.delhiartgallery.com);

Gallery Espace (16 Community Centre, New Friends Colony; tel: 2632 6267; www.gallery espace.com);

Gallery Nature Morte (A1 Neeti Bagh; tel: 4174 0215; www.naturemorte.com);

India Habitat Centre (Lodi Road; tel: 2468 2001; www.indiahabitat.org);

Vadehra Art Gallery (D178, Okhla Phase 1 and D40 Defence Colony; tel: 6547 4005/2461 5368; www.vadehraart.com);

Village Art Gallery (14 Hauz Khas Village; tel: 2685 3860; www.thevillagegallery.co.in).

Right: exhibitions at a commercial art gallery in Hauz Khas.

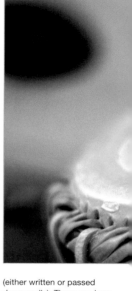

Music and Dance

India's performing arts permeate every aspect of society and culture, forming one of the richest complexes of music, dance and drama of any region of the world. Perhaps most famous in the West for the classical music of the north (also known as Hindustani music), there is also a separate, though related, classical tradition in the south (known as Karnatak music) and a myriad of dance traditions. Delhi, as the capital, attracts performers from all over the country and so there is, uniquely in India, a chance to take in all the different classical dance and music styles, plus a lot more besides.

Hindustani and Karnatak Music

The two classical music traditions of South Asia share certain common ideas and techniques but in presentation, repertory and even instruments they are radically different. Broadly speaking, the classical music culture of the north may be seen as a Muslim tradition, emerging from the Mughal courts. Indeed, many lineages of musicians (family and teaching pedigrees known as *gharanas*) trace their origins back to the famous singer Tansen, who was employed at the court of the Mughal emperor Akhbar (1556–1605).

In contrast, classical musicians in the south are overwhelmingly Hindu and trace their musical roots back to singer-saints of the 17th and 18th centuries. The three most famous of these (the 'musical trinity') are Tyagaraja (1767–1847), Syama Sastri (1772–1827) and Muttusvami Diksitar (1775–1835), whose compositions still form the backbone of Karnatak repertory.

As well as its impressive classical musical heritage India is also home to numerous local performance genres, many of which are intimately tied in with the wider functioning of South Asian society. Due to its inherently auspicious nature, sound, and especially music, is used to mark calendrical festivals and rituals, such as Holi *(see Festivals and Events, p.46)*, as well as being used in the worship of local deities. Weddings are one of the occasions that demand music, and there is a complex set of songs and processional music – usually performed by brass bands playing film songs – that is used as part of the celebrations. Women, in particular, provide songs for many life-cycle rites of passage, including birth and death.

Raga and *Tala*

The works of these singer-saints also show a further difference between the two traditions. In general Hindustani music is improvised while Karnatak music is dependent on compositions

(either written or passed down orally). There are, however, two concepts that they share, *raga* and *tala*, the first dealing the organisation of pitch, the second with the organisation of rhythm and musical time.

Ragas are collections of notes (a bit like a Western musical scale) that have a particular musical 'flavour' (the word *raga* comes from the Sanskrit for 'colour') and which must be performed in a certain way and at certain times of day. The names of *ragas*, particularly in the north, often give their name to the 'piece' being performed. Hence, you might hear a musician say they are going to play *Yaman*, *Bhairav* or *Desh* (all popular Hindustani *ragas*). In the south the piece will take its name from the text of the music being performed, although that too will be composed in a specific *raga*.

Tala is used to describe the repeating rhythmic cells (measured by the number of beats) that give the performance a rhythmic form. In the West we are used to hearing

Left: the head of a *tabla*.

too gives the basic material for further improvisation.

Both the vocal and instrumental performances are accompanied by a number of other performers. The most prominent of these is the *tabla* player, who keeps the tempo and marks the *tala* on a pair of small kettledrums, as well as giving a rhythmic counterpoint to the line of the soloist. Also on stage will be a *tambura*, a long lute a little like a four-string *sitar* that keeps a drone throughout the performance. At vocal performances you may also see either a *sarangi* (a short lute played with a bow) or a harmonium, that imitate the line of the soloist.

In the south the dominant form is the *kriti*. This is a devotional song form that grew out of the three-part *kirtana* (the three sections are called *pallavi*, *anupallavi* and *caranam*). The composers of the 'musical trinity' developed the *kirtana* by adding a series of composed variations known as *sangati* to the form. *Kritis* are performed not only by singers but also on the *vina* (a large plucked lute) and sometimes the violin. The violin is said to have been introduced to Karnatak music by Muttusvami Diksitar's brother, Balusvami, and

music with four-beat units (most popular music) or three beats (like a waltz), but in India these can be much more complex, especially in the south, with repeating *talas* of five, seven and eight beats being common. This complexity increases as musicians employ techniques of doubling or tripling the speed of the music within the *tala* (the degree of mental arithmetic needed to perform some of these variations is awe-inspiring).

Genres and Instruments

Indian classical music is dominated by two different vocal genres, *khayal* in the north and *kriti* in the south. While there are numerous other musical forms, these are the two you are most likely to hear performed in concerts. *Khayal* is said to have been invented by Sultan Hussain Sharqi in the 15th century and it comprises two short, contrasting compositions (known as a *bandish* or

ciz) that are used as a vehicle for improvisation. There is also a short, unaccompanied introduction that presents the notes of the *raga* the following performance is to be in.

In the instrumental adaption of *khayal* now familiar to many in the West, the performer (usually on either the *sitar* or *sarod*, both plucked lutes) gives a longer introduction, an *alap*, adopted from the more austere – and highly valued – vocal genre *dhrupad*. This presents a highly worked out presentation of the *raga*, introducing each note in turn. The instrumental version of the *bandish* or *ciz* that follows is known as a *gat*, and this

Right: adjusting the sound of a *tambura*.

Left: the pellet bells of a *kathak* dancer.

temple). This outraged Victorian sensibilities and an 'anti-nautch campaign' (from the Sanskrit *naca* for dance) eventually ended up with the dancers being banned from temples in 1947.

At the same time a Brahman dancer and teacher, Rukmini Devi, sought to put elements of the dance on stage to promote an indigenous cultural identity in the run-up to Independence. It is this solo dance, accompanied by an ensemble of Karnatak music, that is now seen on the concert stage. The dance draws on both abstract movements (known as *nrtta*) and movement and facial expressions to show emotion *(nrtya)*.

A form with a similar history is *Odissi*. This dance derives from the temple dancers at the Jagannath temple in Puri, Orissa. In 1950, following the ban on temple dance, a group of scholars met to reinvent the tradition for performance on the stage, typically – as is sometimes the way with academics – taking their ideas not from the dancers who were still alive but from temple sculpture and paintings.

The most popular classical dance in the north is *kathak*. Closely linked to the rise of Hindustani music at the North Indian courts – particularly the 'light' forms of *khayal*, *thumri* and *dadra* – it was traditionally danced by courtesans. The dance itself is characterised by fast pirouettes and rhythmic patterns created by the sound of the pellet bells worn around the dancers' ankles.

SEE ALSO LITERATURE AND THEATRE, P.73

While all music in India is, at least theoretically, seen as being auspicious and so in some way devotional, there are certain types of performance which are used explicitly in praise of deities or for use in temples. Not restricted to Hinduism, there are songs from the Sikhs' holy book, the Guru-Granth-Sahib, known as *kirtan* and Muslim devotional songs known as *qavvali*, although these are more often heard in neighbouring Pakistan.

The most widespread devotional form, however, that you are likely to encounter is the Hindu *bhajan*. This is a collective song form usually performed in temples. Often the text is limited to a repetition of the name of the deity being praised and the performance is usually of call-and-response singing. The standard accompaniment is of a *dholak* (a small barrel drum), small pairs of cymbals (usually called *tal*) and a harmonium. While *bhajan* performances are generally given by groups of non-professional devotees there are professional *bhajan* groups who have made numerous recordings and even a sub-genre of pop-*bhajans* with a strong rhythmic beat.

is now the most popular accompanying melodic instrument in South India. The rhythmic accompaniment is provided by a large barrel drum called a *mrdangam*.

Classical Dance

As with music, there are a huge number of dance forms in South Asia, some of them still undocumented. From these a select few have been identified as 'classical' dances – those with long and identifiable histories and with a body of laws *(sastras)* that govern their performance. The earliest textual source for South Asian performance traditions is the *Natyasastra*, thought to have been written by the sage Bharata in around AD 100–200. In it he describes the practice of music, dance and theatre.

The style now known as *bharatanatyam* grew out of Tamil temple dance. The female dancers, called *devadasis*, would perform for the deity as part of temple rituals. Although the dancers were considered to be married to the deity, they took as sexual partners the temple priests or local king (the patron of the

Film Music

The popular music of India par excellence is film song *(filmi git)*. It is heard almost everywhere, from the backs of rickshaws, to shops, to temples playing songs from devotional films (known as 'mythologicals'), as well as in the cinema itself. The first Indian 'talkie' was *Alam Ara*, made in Mumbai in 1931. Based in some respects on traditional Indian theatre, the plot was broken up by songs and dances that pushed the action forward and represented the passing of time. Not only were these early films extremely popular, but so were the songs associated with them, and thus was born India's first pan-Subcontinent popular music.

In the early films the actors and actresses sang themselves, but when recording technology allowed the songs to be dubbed in the late 1930s most film music became prerecorded. It was at this point that specialist 'playback singers' began their rise to superstardom. The biggest of these stars was, and continues to be, Lata Mangeshkar. Along with her sister Asha Bhosle and Geeta Dutt, her high-pitched voice has come to be the ideal female vocal style. Of course the heroine had to have a hero, and the male singers Muhammad Rafi and Mukesh became as idolised as Lata and Asha.

The composers who write the songs, known as 'music directors', command huge payments and are almost as famous as the singers. While early music directors based their songs on traditional Muslim genres such as *ghazal* and *thumri*, soon composers such as the duo Shanker-Jaikishan, S.D. Burman and the brothers Kalyanji Anandji, were bringing ever more eclectic influences to bear on the music. These ranged from *bhajans* to jazz and Latin music to Western pop and rock. Particularly influential were Western film scores like those for the Blaxploitation movie *Shaft* or the TV series *Mission Impossible*. Contemporary music directors, such as the highly sought-after A.R. Rahman, are now global names, the music spreading through extensive NRI (non-resident Indian) communities or, in the case of Rahman, his music making it to London's West End stage through his musical *Bollywood Dreams*, as well as winning him an Oscar for his *Slumdog Millionaire* soundtrack.

SEE ALSO FILM, P.48; LITERATURE AND THEATRE, P.73

Popular Music

Until recently popular music in India was completely dominated by film songs from Bollywood and South Indian movies. While this still forms the vast bulk of the popular music heard in the country there is a small but steadily growing indigenous pop, rock and dance music scene, prompted in part by the arrival of MTV on Indian televisions. Largely based in the major cities, such as Delhi, it has its greatest following amoung the newly wealthy young middle class. On the dance scene *bhangra* continues to attract a following, with many of the artists coming from NRI communities in places like the UK.

Venues and Organisations

For Indian music and dance:
India Habitat Centre
Lodi Road; tel: 2468 2001; www.indiahabitat.org; metro: Jor Bagh; map p.137 D1
India International Centre
40 Max Müller Marg; tel: 2461 9431; www.iicdelhi.nic.in; metro: Jor Bagh; map p.137 D2
Kamani Auditorium
1 Copernicus Marg; tel: 4350 3351; www.kamaniauditorium.org; metro: Mandi House; map p.137 D4
Sangeet Natak Akademi
Rabindra Bhavan, Firoz Shah Road; tel: 2338 7246; www.sangeetnatak.com; metro: Mandi House; map p.137 D4
Triveni Kala Sangam
205 Tansen Marg; tel: 2371 8833; metro: Mandi House; map p.137 D4
For Western music:
The Delhi Music Society
8 Nyaya Marg, Chanakyapuri; tel: 2611 5331; metro: Race Course; map p.136 B2

Right: a band plays at @Live, Connaught Place, *see p.28.*

Pampering

The Indian spa phenomenon came rather late to Delhi, having started in the south, especially Kerala, with *ayurvedic* packages being offered by hotels. However, the concept has now well and truly taken hold with some world-class spas patronised by the city's 'great and good'. They are good places to try out traditional Indian beauty treatments based on the herbal lore of *ayurvedic* medicine; an *ayurvedic* massage with scented, medicated oils can be blissful. There are also an increasing number of beauty products available which draw on *ayurvedic* principles, often very gentle and delightfully fragrant.

The traditional Indian system of healing known as *ayurveda* is said to be based on the teachings contained in the Vedas (Hindu holy scriptures). Using a combination of herbs, oils, massage and meditation, often over a series of days or weeks, its practitioners claim to heal and put the elements of the body back into balance. Most visitors, however, undergo shorter treatments which often amount to no more than a pleasant massage with scented oils, or a herbal face pack. Many spas in Delhi offer 'ayurvedic' packages, and ones you are likely to encounter include such treatments as *dhara* (medicated oils dripped on you), *kizhi* (warm bags containing herbs place upon the body), *pizhichil* (cloth soaked in oils laid over the body), *sirovasti* (similar to *dhara*) and *sukhatiruummu* (a massage with oils).

Spas

The Aman
Lodi Road, Nizamuddin West; tel: 4363 3333; www.aman resorts.com; daily 8am–9pm; metro: JLN Stadium; map p.137 D2

The latest of the hotel spas to open up in Delhi, and it looks set to be one of the best. The gentle wood-and-stone colours are supremely relaxing, and the spa includes steam baths, treatment areas, a bamboo-planted relaxation area and a beauty salon.

The Amatrra Spa @ Ashok
Ashok, Diplomatic Enclave, Chanakyapuri; tel: 2412 2921; www.amatrraspa.com; daily 9am–9pm; metro: Race Course; map p.136 B2

Delhi's most prestigious spa is huge, as is the range of treatments. Whatever they mean by 'Astroayurveda' can only be guessed at, but you will come out feeling relaxed and pampered to within an inch of your life. It also runs fitness programmes, and there is a good pool if you fancy a swim. The Amatrra has its own range of products which you can buy at the spa.

The Amatrra Spa @ Le Meridien
Le Meridien Hotel, 8 Windsor Place, Janpath; tel: 2371 0101; www.amatrraspa.com; daily 9am–10pm; metro: Patel Chowk; map p.137 C3

This is the second of the Amatrra spas in Delhi, and just as well run, relaxing and popular as that at the Ashok. This one is smaller and more intimate, but, like the one at the Ashok, not cheap, and membership here is rarer than hens' teeth.

Asian Roots
B5/15 Safdarjung Enclave; tel: 4610 3000; www.myasian roots.com; Mon–Thur 10am–7pm, Fri–Sun 10am–8pm; metro: Green Park; map p.138 B4

One of the few non-hotel day spas to have started up in Delhi. Very friendly and nicely low-key, it takes its treatments from pan-Asian traditions, which chime with the minimalist East Asian-inspired interior.

Aura at The Park
The Park Hotel, 15 Sansad Marg; tel: 2374 3000; www.theparkhotels.com; daily 8am–9pm; metro: Rajiv Chowk; map p.137 C4

Right: an *ayurvedic* treatment often includes massage with scented oils.

Left: lie back and enjoy
the experience.

metro: Lajpat Nagar; map ref:
p.139 D4
This range of herbal handmade soaps and scrubs is
Fragrant and gentle on the
skin, they are well worth
looking out for. Available from
some branches of Spencer's
Supermarkets.

Fabindia
Central Hall, above Shops 20–
21, Khan Market; tel: 4368 3100;
www.fabindia.com; daily 10am–
8pm; metro: Khan Market; map
p.137 D2
Fabindia has a nice line in its
own toiletries and cosmetics.
Gentle and based on herbal
remedies, the hand- and
bodycreams are very good.
Also at: B28 Connaught Place; 5, 7
and 14 N Block Market, Greater
Kailash I; Karol Bagh, Lajpat Nagar
and Vasant Kunj.

Good Earth
18 Santushti Shopping Arcade;
tel: 2410 0108; www.goodearth
india.com; Mon–Sat 10am–
6.30pm; metro: Race Course;
map p.136 B2
Good Earth has a 'Home
Spa' range that includes
great ayurvedic-inspired
products from Amritam, as
well as essential-oils-based
products from Abahna.
Also at Khan Market and Select
Citywalk Mall, Saket.

Beautifully designed and
chic, the spa at The Park is
great for more mainstream
treatments, including olive oil
massages and excellent
facials. A good choice for
those who are not so keen on
the ayurvedic approach.

Shangri-La Hotel
19 Ashoka Road; tel: 4119 1919;
www.shangri-la.com; daily
7am–11pm; metro: Patel
Chowk; map p.137 C3
Warmer in feel and perhaps
less intimidating than the
Amatrra spas, the Shangri-La
is a great place to be cos-
seted. It offers Asian-based
treatments, but without the

mumbo-jumbo that inevitably
seems to accompany them.

Lotions and Potions
Biotique
29A Khan Market; tel: 2462 2056;
www.biotique.com; Mon–Sat
10.30am–6.30pm; metro: Khan
Market; map p.137 D2
These were some of the first
mass-market ayurveda-
based products to become
available, and they still have
a loyal following for their gentle and fragrant soaps and
creams.

Earthy Goods
C120 Lajpat Nagar; tel: 4608
9562; www.earthygoods.co.in;

Parks and Gardens

There are numerous parks in the city which you can use to escape from the rush of Delhi's streets. Particularly good for children to run around in, as well as to give adults some relaxation, they can also be good for picnics (provided the weather is not too hot). The parks are also important for the ecology of the city: Delhi has one of the highest concentrations of bird species of any city in the world, and its parks are good places for birdspotters to head for to watch their feathered friends.

Connaught Place

Central Park
Connaught Place; daily sunrise–sunset; free; metro: Rajiv Chowk; map p.137 D4
The centre of the circle of Connaught Place is a small park, now remodelled after the works of the metro were removed. It has become a popular meeting place for young people (see box, right).

Talkatora Garden
Willingdon Crescent; daily 3–6pm; free; metro: Jhandewalan; map p.136 B4
These beautifully maintained gardens are on the site of an old tank (tal is Hindi for tank). They are famous for their flowering shrubs in season and are also the location of the Talkatora Indoor Stadium.

Old Delhi and Raj Ghat

Mahatma Gandhi Park
Church Mission Road, Old Delhi; daily sunrise–sunset; free; metro: Chandni Chowk; map p.135 D3
Initially laid out by the British behind the old Town Hall, this small green space is a pleasant respite from the

Above: even Connaught Place has its own park.

bustle of the Old Delhi streets. At the centre of the park is a statue of Gandhi, after whom it was named following Independence.

Raj Ghat
Mahatma Gandhi Marg; daily sunrise–sunset; free; metro: Pragati Maidan; map p.135 E2
Along the banks of the Yamuna are the places where the leaders of Independent India have been cremated. Between the monuments is a huge area of parkland, stretching from the

The park at the centre of the circle of Connaught Place, where the metro entrance is located, has recently been cleaned up and has become a popular meeting place. However, in September 2008 a bomb exploded here, one of a wave across the city, killing a number of people and wounding many others. Although life returned to normal within a few days, there have been calls for much greater security in Delhi's public spaces.

sports centre near Firoz Shah Kotla in the south to Salimgarh Fort in the north. The Shanti Vana ('forest of peace') is a particularly lovely place for a walk.
SEE ALSO MONUMENTS, P.75

North Delhi

Qudsia Bagh
Lala Hardev Sahai Marg, Kashmere Gate; daily sunrise–sunset; free; metro: Kashmere Gate; map p.135 D4
Heading north from Kashmere Gate, immediately behind the unlovely Inter-State Bus terminal, lies the

Left: woodland covers Mehrauli Archaeological Park, *see p.101.*

emperor Aurangzeb was crowned. The gardens are now a little scruffy, but there are a couple of Mughal-era pavilions that are worth taking in if you are planning a trip up north to the Durbar Ground.

Tilak Park
Lala Hardev Sahai Marg, Kashmere Gate; daily sunrise–sunset; free; metro: Kashmere Gate; map p.135 D3

This park is opposite the **Nicholson Cemetery** and was once called Nicholson Park. It was renamed after Independence and it mostly serves as somewhere to kill time while waiting at the Inter-State Bus terminal at Kashmere Gate.

Rajpath and Chanakyapuri

Buddha Jayanti Park
Ridge Road; daily 5am–7pm; free; metro: Shivaji Stadium; map p.136 A3

Set on the Ridge, this lovely park makes quite a contrast with the surrounding scrub, with its lawns and shady trees. The park was laid out to commemorate the 2,500th anniversary of the enlightenment of the Buddha, and its star attraction is a tree that

once magnificent Qudsia Bagh. Built by Qudsia Begum in 1748 for her lover and later husband, the Moghul emperor Muhammad Shah, it originally contained a palace, mosque, canals, waterfalls, rose gardens and fruit trees. While it still retains a peaceful dignity, much of the site was taken over by the bus terminal, and today the buildings and tennis courts have been commandeered by the Masonic Lodge. Under the British, the park was open to Indians only in the morning, reserved for tennis-playing Europeans after midday.

Roshanara Bagh
Roshanara Road; daily sunrise–sunset; free; metro: Pratap Nagar; map p.134 B4

A kilometre (⅝ mile) west of the Ridge Road, just off the main Trunk Road, lies Roshanara Garden, built by Emperor Shah Jahan's youngest daughter as a pleasure garden and site for

Right: Qudsia Bagh is still a pleasant place to while away an hour or so.

her own tomb. Much modified from the elegant original, the park is now home to the Roshanara Club and boasts a well-maintained cricket pitch. The British did away with many of the original monuments, so today only **Roshanara's tomb** itself is still standing.

SEE ALSO MONUMENTS, P.77

Shalimar Bagh
Shalimar Bagh Road, Shalimar Bagh; daily sunrise–sunset; free; metro: Adarsh Nagar

To the north, to the west of the Coronation Memorial, is this garden laid out by Shah Jahan in 1653. Of historic importance, it was where the

Above: mature trees and monuments dot Lodi Gardens.

comes from a cutting of the Bodhi Tree in Sri Lanka, that itself is said to come from a cutting from the original tree under which the Buddha achieved *nirvana*.

The Central Ridge Reserved Forest

From Tughlaqabad to north of the Civil Lines; daily sunrise–sunset; free; metro: Shivaji Stadium; map p.136 A2–B4

The Ridge is a vast area of scrubland preserved right in the centre of Delhi. This rocky terrain, part of the Aravalli hills that run down into Rajasthan, is home to more than 100 species of birds as well as monkeys, the Indian hare and small rodents. There are narrow paths leading into the forest from Sardar Patel Marg, which runs along the side of Chanakyapuri. Once inside the forest you can follow the horse tracks, which run like a maze through the acacia trees. The most common bird on the Ridge is the peacock, while the thorny bushes of the scrub produce berries that attract other species, and you will see raptors soaring above the ridge looking for prey. During March it is worth a visit to see the orange flowers of the flame-of-the-forest trees.

While the Ridge remains the largest tract of open land in the city, it is best to be careful when exploring, do not venture up there on your own and stick to the late morning and early afternoon (between about 10am–4pm).

India Gate Park

India Gate, Rajpath; daily sunrise–sunset; free; metro: Pragati Maidan; map p.137 D3

These very central gardens are particularly good for children as they have an area set aside with climbing frames, swings and slides.

Nehru Park

Panchsheel Road, Chankyapuri; daily sunrise–sunset; free; map p.136 B1

Chanakyapuri's answer to Lodi Gardens. This well-laid-out parkland has mature trees and lush grass. It is a favourite for runners and walkers early in the morning and is a good place to retreat to with a picnic after some heavy shopping at the nearby **Santushti Complex**.

SEE ALSO SHOPPING, P.121

Rashtrapati Bhavan Mughal Gardens

Rashtrapati Bhavan, Vijay Chowk; www.presidentofindia.nic.in; metro: Central Secretariat; map p.136 B3

The huge formal Mughal-style gardens of Rashtrapati Bhavan are among the finest in Delhi but are only open to the public a few times a year (see the website above for more details).

Lodi Gardens and Nizamuddin

Lodi Gardens

Lodi Road; daily sunrise–sunset; free; metro: Jor Bagh; map p.137 D2

This is one of the most beautiful and best-maintained parks in the city, dotted with

Delhi's parks and gardens, like Lodi Gardens, the Garden of Five Senses and the grounds of the Purana Qila, are often used by young couples to meet up and get some privacy away from the prying eyes of their families. It is still frowned on for young Indians to have a boy- or girlfriend, and the couples you sometimes stumble across will often be meeting in secret and, especially for the girl, taking a considerable social risk.

the tombs of the 15–16th-century Lodi rulers. The gardens are beloved by Delhiites who relish the respite it affords from the rush and pollution of the surrounding streets. In the morning you will see people running and walking in the gardens, and later on it becomes a meeting ground for young couples *(see box, left)*. If you are looking for peace and quiet it is perhaps best to avoid the gardens on public holidays, when they are full of picnicking families and are crowded and noisy.

SEE ALSO MONUMENTS, P.79

South Delhi

Hauz Khas Deer Park
Hauz Khas Village; daily sunrise–sunset; free; metro: Green Park; map p.138 B3
Just as you come into Hauz Khas Village, on your right-hand side is the entrance to the Deer Park. This is home to a herd of deer, similar in appearance to those that populate London's Richmond Park. Their diet is markedly different, however; a popular pastime involves buying a *mala*, or garland, of marigolds from the stall opposite the temple on the road that leads to Haus Khaz Village, and then unstringing them and throwing them through the fence to the flower-devouring deer.

This is a good place to bring children; there is a separate play area, and as well as the deer there are rabbits, guinea pigs and peacocks in the park.

Mehrauli
The Garden of the Five Senses
Said-ul-Ajaib, Mehrauli–

Right: in the Garden of the Five Senses.

Badarpur Road; www.delhi tourism.nic.in; daily 8am–9pm; entrance charge; metro Mehrauli
Laid out by Delhi Tourism and opened in 2003, the extensive formal gardens are quite beautiful and full of running water and sculptures. The higher parts of the hill against which they are laid out have been left to the natural scrub of the area, and there are great views over the city.

Mehrauli Archaeological Park
Mehrauli Archaeological Park, Mehrauli Village; daily sunrise–sunset; free; `map p.138 B1
The monuments of Mehrauli are dotted around a wooded area that is now protected as a park, making a very pleasant place to stroll around.

SEE ALSO MONUMENTS, P.81; WALKS, P.131

101

Politics

When India gained its independence from Britain in 1947, Delhi retained its status as the capital, and – for all India's federal structure – as the centre of politics, playing a major part in most of the major political dramas of the last 60 years. Delhi is a political town, its architecture dominated by the monuments of its rulers, past and present, and the streets of New Delhi are regularly brought to a standstill by demonstrations or the cavalcade of minister, chief minister or visiting dignitary. Delhi's press is also full of politics, reports of arm-twisting and machinations liberally sprinkled with political acronyms.

Jawaharlal Nehru

The person who took over the reins of power from the British in 1947 was Jawaharlal Nehru of the Congress Party. As leader of a new country he faced considerable difficulties: the upheavals of Partition left gaping wounds in Indian society that needed to be healed, and there was also the sticky question of how to persuade the nominally independent Princely States of the maharajas to join the new republic. This task he left to his home minister, Sardar Vallabhai Patel, whose right-wing Hindu sensibilities endeared him to the Hindu rulers of Rajasthan.

Nehru put into place a huge programme of industrialisation, at the expense, some might say, of India's overwhelmingly rural population. However, he was determined to bring the country, left in a dire economic state by the British, into the modern world. A Socialist by instinct, he set in place large nationalised industries, fuelled by power from large hydroelectric projects.

Above: Jawaharlal Nehru.

Indira Gandhi and the Emergency

On Nehru's death in 1964 power passd briefly to Lal Bahadur Shastri, before Nehru's daughter, Indira Gandhi, took over in 1966. Initially she was extremely popular, especially after the Bangladesh War of 1971. However, corruption scandals and the poor state of the economy severely reduced her support. Calls for her resigna-

At midnight on 15 August 1947 (Independence Day itself) the new prime minister, Jawaharlal Nehru, rose in the central chamber of Sansad Bhavan to take power of Independent India formally. His stirring speech is one of the most famous made by any Indian politician: 'Long years ago we made a tryst with destiny, and the time comes when we shall redeem our pledge, not wholly or in full measure, but very substantially. At the stroke of the midnight hour, when the world sleeps, India will awake to life and freedom.'

tion grew stronger until, on 26 June 1975, she declared a State of Emergency. She imposed stringent economic measures, which did help a bit, but she also imprisoned her political enemies and handed over much power to her hated son Sanjay.

When she finally called elections in 1977 she was comprehensively beaten by the coalition Janata Party under Moraji Desai. This was riven with internal bickering,

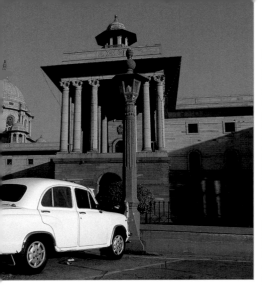

Left: North Block with a ministerial Ambassador.

vinced that the middle class had done sufficiently well to put them back into power. However, they had not counted on the vast majority of Indians who continue to live in abject poverty. The BJP was trounced and the Congress won, due in part to the role played by Rajiv Gandhi's widow, Sonia.

She turned down the offer of becoming prime minister, letting that instead go to the respected Manmohan Singh, but continues to wield considerable influence in Congress politics. The Nehru-Gandhi dynasty continues to fascinate India, and now Sonia's son Rahul is beginning to take an ever larger part in politcal life. He is being tipped for high office, a fact recognised in public by Manmohan Singh in 2010, although it will not be until the next general elections, due to be held by 2014, that Rahul's ambitions will really be known.

though, and when elections were called again in 1980, Indira and Congress swept back into power.

She was faced, though, by calls for an independent Sikh homeland in the Punjab. When she sent troops into the Golden Temple in Amritsar to flush out some militants, the desecration of the shrine caused great anger in the Sikh community. On 31 October 1984 she was assassinated by her own Sikh bodyguards outside her house on Sardarjang Road. The brutal anti-Sikh riots that swept the city killed over 2,000 people.

Into her shoes stepped her younger son, Rajiv Gandhi, although his fate was to be similar to his mother's. In 1991 he was blown up by a Tamil suicide bomber opposed to India's intervention in the civil war in Sri Lanka.

The Rise of the Hindu Right

Congress continued to hold on to power under the veteran politician Narasimha Rao, but his government was beset by corruption scandals.

The main beneficiary was the BJP, a right-wing Hindu party that had grown out of the Janata Party of the 1970s. It was briefly part of a minority government in 1989, but this fell when the leader of the BJP, L.K. Advani, embarked on a countrywide crusade to raise support for the destruction of the Babri Masjid in Ayodhya, said to have been built on the birthplace of Rama. In 1992 hundreds of militant Hindus destroyed the mosque, and there ensued some of the worst communal rioting ever seen by India.

However, they were soon back in power, becoming the largest party in 1996, and then forming a coalition goverment from 1998–2004. During this time Prime Minister Atal Vajpayee shocked the world by conducting tests of nuclear weapons and then by nearly going to war with Pakistan over the continually disputed region of Kashmir.

India Shining?

At the 2004 election, the BJP and its allies ran on a message of 'India Shining', con-

Indian politicians and the media love a good acronym, and many political parties are known simply by their initials. The BJP is the opposition, the right-wing Hindu Bharatiya Janata Party. The CPI is the Communist Party of India, not to be confused with the CPI(M), which is the Communist Party of India (Marxist). Then there is the BSP, the Bahujan Samaj Party that champions the low castes led by Mayawati Kumari. There are also regional parties the TDP, Telugu Desam Party from Andhra Pradesh, and the bitter rivals DMK and AIADMK from Tamil Nadu, whose full Tamil names are real tongue-twisters.

Religions and Religious Sites

Delhi is home to representatives of all of India's many religions, and each has left its mark on the city through its places of worship. These range from large, impressive mosques and Hindu temples, to historic churches, to the amazing lotus-shaped temple of the Baha'is. Places of worship, for all religions, have varying opening times; those below are a guide only, and they depend greatly on the time of year and festivals. None charges an entrance fee, but it is customary to leave a small donation when leaving.

Above: the Lakshmi Narayan Mandir, *see p.106.*

Above: the Lakshmi Narayan Mandir, *see p.106.*

Temple Etiquette
When entering a temple, *gurudwara* or mosque you must remove your shoes (there is usually somewhere safe to keep them). Do not take leather items of any kind into a Jain temple. Dress modestly, covering your arms and legs, and in mosques and *gurudwaras* women must cover their heads. When walking around a Hindu or Jain shrine you are expected to walk clockwise.

Delhi's Religions

HINDUISM

There is no one set of beliefs that might sum up India's dominant belief system, Hinduism. No other religious tradition, or group of devotees, is so eclectic; it is not traced to a specific founder and does not have a single holy book as its scriptural authority. There are a plethora of deities, some such as Siva, Vishnu, Brahma and Devi recognised across the country, some only local, that can be worshipped through a tradition of direct devotion (*bhakti*) or by elaborate temple rituals derived from the Vedic scriptures. The land and landscape of India is intimately entwined with Hindu beliefs, from bathing in holy rivers such as the Ganga, to Kailash the holy mountain of Siva, to sacred groves of trees.

ISLAM

Islam is a religion derived from the revelations of the prophet Muhammad. These are claimed to have been passed down to him by the Archangel Gabriel and they now form the text of the Muslim holy book, the Qur'an, which builds on the texts of the Jews and Christians. It is upon this text that Muslims base their lives. In order to be a good Muslim one must follow five basic precepts and practices: to assert that there is no God but Allah, and Muhammad is his Prophet; to pray, preferably five times a day; to perform acts of charity; to observe a fast from dawn to dusk throughout the month of Ramadan; to go on a pilgrimage to Makkah (Mecca) at least once during one's lifetime.

Left: Old Delhi's impressive Jama Masjid, *see p.107*.

Mahavira ('great hero'), was an elder contemporary of the Buddha. The two teachers had much in common: both were Kshatriyas of royal descent but renounced the worldly life; both rejected caste barriers and questioned the sacredness of the Vedas (early Hindu scriptures).

The concept of a deity has little or no place in Jainism. The popular deities of Hinduism are accepted, but they are given less significance than the *jinas* ('conquerers'), who are regarded as the true focus of devotion. Mahavira is said to be the last of a line of 24 *jinas*, also known as *tirthankaras* ('crossing-makers'), who attained perfect wisdom *(kaivalya)* through different penances, to vanquish desire and break their bonds with the material world.

THE SIKHS

The process of bringing Hinduism and Islam close to each other was set in train by the gurus Kabir and Nanak. Born into a Brahmin family, Kabir was brought up by Muslim foster parents. He was a disciple of Ramananda, a famous Hindu saint, but he was also deeply influenced by Sufism and used Sufi terminology in many of his poems. Inspired by Kabir, Guru Nanak (1469–1539) founded the Sikh religion with the avowed purpose of synthesising Hinduism and Islam.

The 10th guru, Govind Singh, transformed the pacifist Sikh sect into a martial community, so it could defend itself against persecution. He introduced rites of initiation into a well-organised Sikh brotherhood known as the *Khalsa*. Govind Singh also decided to terminate the succession of gurus. He asked his followers to look upon their holy book, the Granth Sahib, as the sole object of veneration, and so it became the symbol of God.

BUDDHISM AND JAINISM

The Buddha was born in India in around 563 BC, and until his death in circa 483 BC he travelled extensively, disseminating his teaching to disciples. While initially Buddhism became popular, there are now very few Buddhists in India. However, at about the same time as the Buddha was preaching, another religious tradition was being established. Vardhamana, better known by his title

CHRISTIANITY

There have been Christians in South India since at least the 4th century AD. However, Christianity in the north of the country took hold only once European colonial missionaries began to proselytise in India from around the beginning of the 19th century. Many converts were low-

James Skinner was born in 1778 to a Scottish father and a Hindu mother, and because of his mixed birth he was not allowed into the British Army. So he joined the armies of the Marathas and formed his own cavalry unit under the Maharaja of Gwalior. When the Marathas turned to fighting the British, Skinner switched sides and was allowed to form his own cavalry, which became known as 'Skinner's Horse', and it still forms part of the Indian Army. Skinner died in 1841 and was buried in St James's.

Above: St James's Church in the Civil Lines, *see p.108*.

caste Hindus seeking to escape the strictures of the caste system.

Connaught Place

Bangla Sahib Gurudwara
Baba Kharak Singh Marg; daily 2.30–9.30pm; metro: Patel Chowk; map p.136 C4

The main Sikh temple in Delhi is reminiscent of Amritsar's Golden Temple, although without the actual gold. The *gurudwara* is dominated by a large central pool, in the middle of which lies the temple itself. Round-the-clock recitals of the Granth Sahib, the faith's holy book, lend a special atmosphere, and all visitors are offered free food, but they may be asked to help out in the kitchen.

Hanuman Mandir
Baba Kharak Singh Marg; daily morning and evening; metro: Rajiv Chowk; map p.137 C4

At first sight this is not an especially architecturally distinguished Hindu temple, but it was built by Jai Singh (he of the Jantar Mantar) in the early 18th century. It is very popular and dedicated to the monkey-god who helped Rama in his fight against Ravanna. It is especially busy on Tuesdays, when many

devotees come to pay their respects.

Jhandewalan Hanuman Mandir
Link Road, Jhandewalan; daily morning and evening; metro: Jhandewalan; map p.134 B2

This temple is marked by a huge new pink statue of Hanuman, close to the metro station. In a piece of jaw-dropping kitsch, during the evening *puja* the statue opens its arms and out from its chest pop statues of Rama and Sita; it has to be seen to be believed. The entrance to the temple is almost as good as you walk through the open jaws of a vanquished demon.

Kali Bari Mandir
Mandir Marg; daily morning and evening; metro: R.K. Ashram Marg; map p.134 B1

This small temple sits next door to the Lakshmi Narayan Mandir and is dedicated to the goddess in one of her more fierce aspects. Kali is especially worshipped in Kolkata, and this temple is patronised by the Bengali community of Delhi.

Lakshmi Narayan Mandir
Mandir Marg; daily sunrise–sunset; metro: R.K. Ashram Marg; map p.134 B1

Officially known as Lakshmi Narayan Mandir, but often referred to as Birla Mandir after industrialist Raja Birla, who financed its construction in 1938, this is one of the finest examples of Hindu temple architecture in Delhi. Built in the decorative Orissan style, and dedicated to Lakshmi, the goddess of well-being, it is very popular with locals and visitors alike. The temple was opened by Gandhi on the condition that it should be open to all regardless of their background.

Sacred Heart Cathedral
Ashoka Road and Baba Kharak Singh Marg; daily morning and evening; metro: Patel Chowk; map p.136 C4

Henry Medd's Sacred Heart Cathedral is the city's principal Catholic place of worship. Its painted, cake-icing exterior is well maintained, as is the more austere interior. St Francis looks down from the rooftop.

St Thomas's Church
Mandir Marg; Sun sunrise–sunset; metro: R.K. Ashram Marg; map p.134 C1

Right: the *dargah* of Nizamuddin Auliya, *see p.109*.

This fabulous Modernist red-brick church was designed by the architect Walter George and built in 1930–32. Well worth a look if you are in the area, it makes a nice contrast to the ornate Lakshmi Narayan Mandir nearby.

Old Delhi and Raj Ghat

Baptist Church

Chandni Chowk, opposite Sisganj Gurudwara; Sun sunrise–sunset; metro: Chandni Chowk; map p.135 D3

Although the external appearance of this church has been altered over the years, it is one of the earliest Christian places of worship in Delhi and retains much of its original interior. It was built in 1814 by the Baptist Missionary Society and is still in use. It is generally only open on Sunday, but if you can track down the caretaker he will let you look around inside.

Fatehpuri Masjid

Chandni Chowk; daily sunrise–sunset; metro: Chandni Chowk; map p.135 C3

At the western end of Chandni Chowk is this elegant red sandstone mosque. It was built in 1650 on the instructions of Begum Fatehpuri, a wife of Shah Jahan. It has a central dome with two

flanking *chatris* (open pavilions) and two minarets on the corners of the façade.

Jain Mandir and Bird Hospital

Chandni Chowk; daily 8am–8pm; metro: Chandni Chowk; map p.135 D3

This is the oldest Jain temple in Delhi. It was built in 1658 out of red sandstone, and hence its other name, the Lal (Red) Mandir. The image in the central sanctum of the temple is that of Parsvanath, the 23rd of the 24 *tirthankaras*. Attached to the temple is the Bird Hospital, where birds that have been injured are nursed back to health before being released back into the wild.

Jama Masjid

Jama Masjid, Old Delhi; daily winter 7am–12.15pm, 1.45pm–sunset, summer 8.30am–12.15pm, 1.45–sunset, except during prayers; metro: Chandni Chowk; map p.135 D2

The magnificent Jama Masjid is India's largest mosque. The mosque's three gateways, their scale and splendour intended to intimidate and inspire the devout, lead to the 25,000-capacity courtyard. The gate to the east was originally only for use by the emperor and his family, and

even today is open only on Fridays. Such is the mosque's size that the platform in front of the central tank was used by an extra prayer-leader to relay the actions of the imam to the worshippers on the western side too far away to make him out.

There is a small shed on the northwestern side of the courtyard, where for a small fee you'll be shown a hair from the Prophet's beard, a sandal and his footprint. The minaret in the opposite corner can be climbed for a small fee, although women on their own are discouraged from doing so. The views of the top of the Red Fort and New Delhi make the climb more than worthwhile.

St Stephen's Church

Church Mission Road, Old Delhi; Sun sunrise–sunset; metro: Chandni Chowk; map p.135 D3

Built in 1862, this somewhat square neo-Romanesque church is built in red brick, giving rise to the local legend that the colour reflects the blood from the stoning to death of the saint. The stained-glass rose window is worth a look if you are in the area, as it is the only one in Delhi. As with most churches

Above: the extraordinary Baha'i Lotus Temple.

in Delhi, it is open only for worship, but if you ask the caretaker you can have a look inside.

Shahi Idgah
Rani Jhansi Road, Sadar Bazaar; daily sunrise–sunset; metro: Pulbangash; map p.134 C2

This large, enclosed prayer ground is to the west of the Old City. As well as acting as a place of worship, it is also a Muslim burial ground, with a number of graves set around the site. The impressive gateways of the paved grounds are well worth a look. It is thought to date back to the 17th century.

Sisganj Gurudwara
Chandni Chowk; daily 2.30–9.30pm; metro: Chandni Chowk; map p.135 D3

One of the holiest sites for Sikhs in Delhi, the *gurudwara* is on the spot where the ninth guru, Tegh Bahadur, was killed on the orders of the Mughal emperor Aurangzeb. Notable artefacts kept in the *gurudwara* are part of the banyan tree under which he was martyred, as well as the place where he was imprisoned beforehand.

North Delhi
Jhandewalan Devi Mandir
Off Rani Jhansi Road, Karol Bagh; daily morning and evening; metro: Jhandewalan; map p.134 B2

This goddess temple is one of the most venerated in the city. There has been a temple here since at least the time of Shah Jahan, although the current building dates from the 19th century. It takes its name from the flags (*jhandas*) that were flown on this spot.

Majnu ka Tila
NH1 Timapur; daily 2.30–7.30pm; metro: Vishwa Vidyalaya

The large and ornate building of this *gurudwara* dates from the 1980s, but the site has long been holy to the Sikhs as it is connected with the visit of the first guru, Nanak, to Delhi during the 15th century. It is said to derive its name from that of a Muslim hermit who lived on the site and who was shown the path to enlightenment by Guru Nanak.

St James's Church
Church and Lothian roads; daily morning and evening; metro: Kashmere Gate; map p.135 D3

St James's Church was built by James Skinner *(see box on p.106)* in 1836, making it Delhi's oldest surviving church. Legend has it that Skinner was lying wounded on a battlefield when he vowed that if God let him survive, he would build a church. Skinner's grave lies in front of the altar, while his family graveyard is outside, to the north of the church. The church itself is of a classical Western design, the plan is in the Greek Cross configuration. Badly damaged during the Uprising, it underwent restoration work in 1865, and the stained-glass windows were touched up in 1996.

Rajpath and Chanakyapuri
Bhairon Mandir
Bhairon Marg, Purana Qila; daily morning and evening; metro: Pragati Maidan; map p.137 E3

The two popular shrines on this site, by the eastern wall of the Purana Qila, are dedicated to Siva. It is said that

Right: a *puja* in progress; the Kalkaji Mandir, *see p.110*.

there has been a temple here for centuries, but the present buildings show no evidence of that; however, the main images of the Bhairon, Hanuman and Bhima are intriguing – rocks painted silver and orange with large eyes.

Cathedral Church of the Redemption

Church Road, north of Jaipur Column; daily sunrise–sunset; metro: Central Secretariat; map p.136 C3

Built in 1927–35 by one of Edwin Lutyens's students, Henry Medd, this rather sober brick-and-stone Anglican church has an attractive, light-filled interior. The cathedral is noted for its organ and stained-glass windows.

Gurudwara Rakab Ganj

Church Road, by Sansad Bhavan; daily sunrise–sunset; metro: Central Secretariat; map p.136 C3

This impressive white *gurudwara* dates back to 1732 and is said to sit on the spot where the ninth guru, Teg Bahadur, was cremated. The man who rescued the guru's body was named Lakhi Banjara, and it is he who commissioned this building to commemorate the event.

The Bhairon Mandir temple is unusual in that in one of the shrines' offerings are made to Siva in the form of whisky.

Khairul Manazil Masjid

Mathura Road; daily sunrise–sunset; metro: Pragati Maidan; map p.137 D3

Opposite the entrance to the Purana Qila is this mosque built in 1561 by Maham Anga, the mother of Adham Khan, who served at the court of the emperor Akhbar. Although it is now in a very dilapidated condition, some of the original exquisite tiling still remains over the doorways. The mosque is technically still operational, but prayers are only performed here very rarely.

Lodi Gardens and Nizamuddin

Gurudwara Damdama Sahib

Bharat Scouts and Guides Marg; daily 2.30–8pm; metro: JLN Stadium; map p.137 E2

The shiny white dome of this shrine, easily seen from Humayun's Tomb, marks the spot where the last of the Sikh gurus, Gobind Singh,

met the Mughal emperor Bahadur Shah I in 1707. The emperor wanted to stage a fight between his elephant and the guru's, but the guru said that any buffalo of the Punjab would be a match for the elephant. Legend has it that he was right and that the elephant fled.

Nizamuddin's Tomb

Nizamuddin West; daily sunrise–sunset; metro: Jangpura; map p.137 E2

To the east of Humayan's Tomb is the shrine, or *dargah*, of the Sufi saint of the Chisti order, Sheikh Nizamuddin Auliya (1236–1325), after whom the surrounding colonies are named. The *dargah* is a haven of peace in this busy Muslim area; the tomb of the saint is in a pavilion with beautiful marble screens (note that women are not allowed in the tomb itself). Also buried here are the Mughal emperor Muhammad Shah (1719–48) and the saint's disciple and poet Amir Khusrau. On Thursday evenings between 5–7pm *qavvali* is sung at the tomb.

South Delhi

Baha'i Lotus Temple

East of Nehru Place; daily

Above: *kum kum* powder ready for use at the Kalkaji Mandir.

summer 9am–7pm, winter 9.30am–5.30pm; metro: Kalkaji Mandir; map p.139 E3

Directly south of Nizamuddin is the modern white marble, lotus-shaped Baha'i Lotus Temple. Standing on Kalkaji Hill, this iconic piece of Delhi architecture was designed by Fariburz Shah and completed in 1986 as a pilgrimage site for the Iranian Baha'i sect. It is set in beautifully maintained gardens, and visitors must take off their shoes before walking through them to the temple itself.

Begumpuri Masjid
Begumpur, Sarvodaya Enclave; daily sunrise–sunset; metro: Malviya Nagar; map p.138 C2

This partly ruined and monumental mosque is the second-largest in the city after the Jama Masjid in Old Delhi. It was built as part of Muhammad bin Tughlaq's city of Jahanpanah. Supposedly built by Khan-e-Jahan Telingani, it is built of stone and rubble, and the walls have a characteristic slope to them. The multi-domed construction has a stately interior dominated by a central arch with soaring minarets.

Chiragh-i-Dilli Dargah
Chirag Delhi; daily sunrise–

sunset; metro: Hauz Khas; map p.139 D2

This is the *dargah* of the Muslim saint Nasir-ud-Din Mahmud, a disciple of Nizamuddin Auliya. the tomb dates back to 1356, and the delicate construction consists of a dome over the central shrine, with a walkway supported by slender columns.

ISKON Temple
Raja Dhirshain Marg; daily 4.30am–noon, 4–7.45pm; metro: Moolchand; map p.139 E3

This is the main Delhi temple for the International Society for Krishna Consciousness (aka the Hare Krishnas). The wedding-cake confection that is the temple itself was built in 1998 and is decorated inside with wall-paintings of the exploits of Krishna and Radha, and Rama and Sita. There are also displays that explain the two main Hindu epics, the *Mahabharata* and *Ramayana*. Close by the temple is an inscription of the edicts of the Buddha by the Mauryan emperor Ashoka.

Kalkaji Mandir
Outer Ring Road, Nehru Place; Tue–Sun morning and evening; metro: Nehru Place

This Hindu temple dedicated to the goddess Kalka Devi was founded as early as 1764, when a farmer is said to have built the temple in honour of a cow that gave all its milk to the goddess. Additions were made during the 19th century, but most parts of the domed, 12-sided building are modern. Relatively unadorned, this temple makes an interesting contrast with its flashier Baha'i neighbour, and comes alive particularly during the festival of Navaratri in October, when thousands of pilgrims flock here.

Right and Far Right: the huge temple complex at Chattarpur.

Khirki Masjid
Press Enclave Marg, Khirki Village; daily sunrise–sunset; metro: Malviya Nagr; map p.139 D1

This extraordinary building was built a little later than the Begumpuri Masjid by Firoz Shah Tughlaq. Similarly monumental, it is set on a raised plinth with arched windows all around with square *jali* work (stone lattice) set into them. The flat roof supports nine sets of nine small domes, and the interior gives way to four courtyards, one for each quadrant of the building.

Moth ki Masjid
Masjid Moth, South Extension II; daily sunrise–sunset; metro: Hauz Khas; map p.139 C3

This lovely mosque, after which the surrounding village is named, dates back to the Lodi period. It is entered through a beautiful sandstone gateway with marble bands with calligraphic inscriptions. The three-domed construction marks it as a forerunner of the Jamali Kamali mosque in Mehrauli and Sher Shah's mosque in the Purana Qila.

Chattarpur, one of the largest Hindu temples in Delhi, is particularly animated during the festival of Navratri (see p.47).

Mehrauli and Tughlaqabad

Chattarpur Temple
Gurgaon–Mehrauli Road; daily morning and evening; metro: Chhatarpur

Visitors keen on temple architecture might like to visit Chattarpur, an area dotted with temples, chief among them Chattarpur Temple itself. Built from white marble and intricately carved in the South Indian style, this Hindu structure has smaller temples within dedicated to Lords Shiva, Ganesha and Rama, but has the goddess Durga as the chief presiding deity.

Dada Bari Jain Temple, Ahinsa Sthal
Mehrauli Village; daily sunrise–sunset; metro: Qutab Minar; map p.138 B1

This relatively modern Jain temple gives a flavour of the ornate decoration to be seen in Jain buildings elsewhere in India. The marble interior is beautifully maintained, and the carved columns and decorated ceiling are exquisite. The temple also contains what is said to be the 800-year-old *samadhi* (mausoleum) of the guru Suruswarji Maharaj.

Not far from the temple, on a small rise on the Gurgaon–Mehrauli Road, is the Ahinsa Sthal. This is a monumental statue of the Jain *tirthankara* Mahavira.

Qutbuddin Bakhtiyar Kaki Dargah and Moti Masjid
Mehrauli Village; daily sunrise–sunset; metro: Qutab Minar; map p.138 B1

The Sufi saint Qutb-ud-din Bakhtiyar Kaki is buried here, and his shrine attracts many devotees, especially on Thursdays and Fridays when *qavvali* are sung here. (Note that women are not allowed inside the tomb itself.)

The marble mosque (Moti Masjid) attached to the *dargah* was commissioned by Bahadur Shah I (the son of Aurangzeb). He is buried in the *dargah* complex, along with two other Mughal emperors, Shah Alam and Akhbar II.

The attractive **Hathi Gate** next to the *dargah* was built by the last Mughal emperor, Bahadur Shah, as an addition to the late-Mughal palace here.

Guragon, Noida and Trans-Yamuna

Akshardham
Noida Mor; www.akshardham.com; Tue–Sun 9am–6pm; metro: Akshardham

One of the more recent additions to Delhi's collection of temples is Akshardham, a spectacular complex inaugurated in 2005. Described as 'an enlightening journey through India's glorious art, values and contributions for the progress, happiness and harmony of mankind', it's a hugely impressive undertaking, with no expense spared in its construction. As well as some exquisite temple architecture, there are also several award-winning multimedia presentations, a musical fountain and a boating lake. It is located on the eastern bank of the Yamuna river, just underneath Nizamuddin Bridge.

Restaurants

Delhi has the widest range and the best restaurants in India. Although there are eating places scattered all over the city, you will find a cluster of good restaurants around Connaught Place, while the five-star hotels in the Diplomatic Enclave, Chanakyapuri, have some of the finest Indian restaurants in the world. Other good hunting grounds close to the centre include Khan Market and the colonies around Lodi Gardens. The middle-class colonies in South Delhi have seen an explosion in decent places to eat, and you will find some excellent Indian, Italian and East Asian food here.

At one time it was possible to walk into almost any restaurant in Delhi and be fairly sure of getting a table, even if you had to wait for a bit. That, at least for the higher end and more trendy places, has changed. Reservations are recommended for almost all of the restaurants listed here, and the more upmarket they are the more necessary it is to book ahead; a local mobile phone is very useful.

Connaught Place

19 Oriental Avenue
Shangri-La Hotel, 19 Ashok Road; tel: 4119 1919; daily noon–3pm, 7–11.45pm; ££££; metro: Patel Chowk; map p.137 C3
This has to be Delhi's top East Asian restaurant, serving first-rate Chinese, Thai and Japanese food. The dim sum is particularly good, if pricey, and there are a few unusual dishes you won't find elsewhere.

Cibo
Hotel Janpath, Janpath; tel: 4302 9291; daily noon–midnight; £££–££££; metro: Patel Chowk; map p.136 C4

Baroque extravagance is the hallmark of this remarkable Mediterranean restaurant, created by the same designer who created **Veda** *(see p.114)*. The indoor seating is pleasant enough, but the outdoor area is exceptional, with a walled garden, flowing water on three sides and a huge bunch of grapes as the centrepiece. The food is equally impressive, with Italian favourites plus some new twists.

Kake Da Hotel
M74, NDMC Market, Connaught Place; tel: 2341 1580; daily noon–11.30pm; £; metro: Rajiv Chowk; map p.137 C4

A simple but well-established and perennially popular Punjabi *dhaba*. The food here is dependably tasty and extremely good value, which, combined with the lightning-quick service, makes this place a winner.

Mist
The Park, 15 Sansad Marg; tel: 2374 3000; daily 24 hours; ££££; metro: Rajiv Chowk; map p.137 C4
The chic 24-hour coffee shop at The Park is a good place to stop off for a light meal – try the pizzas or the South Indian dishes – or a quiet drink. Perhaps the real draw,

Left: modish interior design at Veda, *see p.114.*

Left: the Lodi Garden Restaurant, *see p.117.*

Price per person for an average meal:
£ under Rs 200
££ Rs 200–500
£££ Rs 500–1,000
££££ Over Rs 1,000

though, is the modern designer interior.

Nirula's
K14 Connaught Place; tel: 2341 2868; daily 10.30am–11pm; £; metro: Rajiv Chowk; map p.137 C4

Delhi's own fast-food chain (in locations all over town, but the original Connaught Place outlet is still the favourite, and now looking much fresher after a refit), and considerably better than its foreign rivals. The burgers, pizzas and salads are all tasty, and it remains a good place for breakfast. Better still are the ice creams (a vast range is on offer at the parlour beside the CP restaurant).

Sakura
Metropolitan Hotel, Bangla Sahib Marg; tel: 4250 0200; daily 7–9.30am, noon–2.30pm, 6–11.30pm; ££££; metro: R.K. Ashram Marg; map p.136 C4

Excellent and beautifully presented Japanese food (there is an extensive menu in Japanese), the most authentic to be found in the city. As well as the impressive list of sushi and sashimi there are good wines by the glass. It is not cheap, but the set meals are good value.

Saravana Bhavan
46 Janpath; tel: 2331 7755; daily 8am–11pm; £; metro: Rajiv Chowk; map p.137 C4

One of a chain of excellent vegetarian South Indian restaurants, with good *dosas* and *thalis*. Very clean, good-value and efficient.

The Spice Route
Hotel Imperial, 1 Janpath; tel: 2334 1234; daily 12.30–3pm, 7–11.45pm; ££££; metro: Rajiv Chowk; map p.137 C4

A superb restaurant, beautifully decorated with wooden pillars and carvings. The wall paintings were done by artists from the Keralan temple town of Guruvayur. Fabulous, if pricey, Sri Lankan and Southeast Asian food, but the winner has to be the interior; one of the finest restaurant designs in Delhi.

Ten
10 Sansad Marg, below the YWCA International Guest House; tel: 2374 8026; daily 7.30am–10pm; ££; metro: Patel Chowk; map p.137 C4

This pleasant, quiet restaurant has a good selection of European food, such as pasta and stews, and a few Indian dishes to round out the menu. The desserts are particularly good. It is a nice

Right: the ever-dependable Saravana Bhavan.

place for a leisurely breakfast or brunch.

Veda

H26–27, Connaught Place; tel: 4151 3535; daily noon–3.30pm, 8–11.30pm; £££–££££; metro: Rajiv Chowk; map p.137 C4

Decorated with help from one of Delhi's leading fashion designers, the candlelit, Baroque-style interior sets this place apart from the moment you enter. The inventive modern Indian food is also a break from the norm, though the North Indian dishes are better than those from the south. The wine list is impressive, and the cocktails well put together. Overall, it's expensive but does much to justify the cost.

SEE ALSO CAFÉS AND BARS, P.30

Old Delhi and Raj Ghat

Chor Bizarre

Hotel Broadway, 4/15A Asaf Ali Road; tel: 2327 3821; daily

Price per person for an average meal:
£ under Rs 200
££ Rs 200–500
£££ Rs 500–1,000
££££ Over Rs 1,000

noon–4pm, 7.30–11.30pm; £££; metro: New Delhi; map p.135 D2

Reliably delicious Mughlai and Kashmere fare served in interestingly quirky surroundings. The salad buffet is housed in a classic car, while the tables are made from all manner of oddments, including a four-poster bed. Reservations are highly recommended.

Karim Hotel

Gali Kababiyan, Matia Mahal, near the Jama Masjid; tel: 2326 9880; daily 7am–midnight; £; metro: Chawri Bazar; map p.135 D2

Probably the best Muslim food in the city. Mouthwatering non-vegetarian *tanduri* dishes and excellent breads. It can be a little difficult to find (down a tiny alley on the left walking south from the Jama Masjid), but just ask for directions if you get lost. There are now other, less atmospheric, branches of this legendary restaurant in other parts of the city, including Nizamuddin West and Greater Kailash I.

Moti Mahal Deluxe

3703 Netaji Subhash Marg, Daryaganj; tel: 2327 3011; daily noon–3.30pm, 7pm–midnight;

££–£££; metro: Chandni Chowk; map p.135 D2

Long one of Delhi's standard bearers for North Indian (Punjabi and Mughlai) food, the slightly dingy interior belies the quality of the dishes on offer. If you are after classics such as butter chicken or *murgh masala* it is worth a visit. Now a small chain, the outlets elsewhere in Delhi (try the Diplomatic Enclave, M Block Market in Greater Kailash I or Defence Colony) are a bit less run-down.

North Delhi

Thai Wok

Road 31, Punjabi Bagh Extension, DDA Market; tel: 2522 3469; daily 11am–11pm; £££ metro: Punjabi Bagh

Regrettably, this restaurant has now moved from its once stellar location overlooking the Qutb Minar to Punjabi Bagh Extension in northeast Delhi, the Thai cuisine is still worth a try if you are in the area. Authentically fiery, and with huge portions, it is still one of Delhi's better ventures into Southeast Asian food.

Right: rather unusual features at Chor Bizarre.

Left: curries and kebabs at Karim Hotel.

Rajpath and Chanakyapuri

Basil & Thyme

Santushi Shopping Complex, Chanakyapuri; tel: 2467 4933; daily 10.30am–6pm; £££; metro: Race Course; map p.136 B2

A pleasant and quiet lunch spot, set in a elegantly minimal interior overlooking the lawns of Santushti. It serves good and reasonably priced European food, including excellent quiche and cheesecake.

Bukhara

The ITC Maurya, Sardar Patel Marg, Diplomatic Enclave; tel: 2611 2233; daily 12.30–2.45pm, 7–11.45pm; ££££; metro: Dhaula Kuan; map p.136 A2

Often picked out as serving the best *tanduri* food in the city, this Delhi institution serves up beautifully prepared food from NWFP. The kebabs and *makhni dal* are delicious, attested to by the long list of famous visitors. Booking is essential.

Dum Phukt

The ITC Maurya, Sardar Patel Marg, Diplomatic Enclave; tel: 2611 2233; daily 7–11.30pm, Sat–Sun 12.30–2.45pm; ££££; metro: Dhaula

Aside from discovering the food from the south of their own country, Delhiites have taken to foreign and fusion food with gusto. Heading the list have to be Southeast Asian cuisines, the hot chilli that is often used chiming well with the Indian palate. Next in line, though, is Mediterranean food, particularly Italian. This features on the menus of many of the capital's most trendy cafés, bars and restaurants, complete with drizzled olive oil and sundried tomatoes. Other favourites include Japanese dishes, with sushi being a surprise hit, and 'gastro-fast food' along the lines of burgers, cakes and smoothies.

Kuan; map p.136 A2

The Maurya's other world-class restaurant, serving expensive but exquisite Avadhi dishes. One of the signature dishes is prepared by lengthy steaming in a sealed pot so the food literally melts in your mouth, while the kebabs are to die for. A real taste of old Lucknow; as with the Bukhara, reservations are essential.

Have More

11–12 Pandara Road Market;

tel: 2338 7070; daily noon–1am; ££–£££; metro: Khan Market; map p.137 D2

The handful of up-market *dhabas* here are all reasonable, but this is the best of the bunch. The location of these late-closing Punjabi restaurants so close to India Gate makes them a good place to have lunch while taking in the sights or handy for a late dinner.

Masala Art

Taj Palace, Sardar Patel Marg; tel: 2611 0202; daily 12.30–2.45pm, 6.30–11.45pm; ££££; metro: Dhaula Kuan; map p.136 A2

Modern Indian cuisine reinvented as health food (no heavy *ghi* here, just olive oil and lots of light vegetable dishes). Predictably it is now popular with those who lunch, but the flavoursome food is equally good for dinner.

Olive Beach

Hotel Diplomat, 9 Sardar Patel Marg, Diplomatic Enclave; tel: 4604 0404; daily noon–12.30am; ££££; metro: Central Secretariat; map p.136 A2

This is an offshoot of Olive's Bar & Restaurant in Mehrauli, *(see p.119).* Located in the Hotel Diplomat in the much more reachable Chanakya-

puri district, the food has improved, and it is generally held to be the city's best Mediterranean eatery, particularly famous for its pizzas. Reservations are a must.

Orient Express

Taj Palace, 2 Sardar Patel Marg, New Delhi; tel: 2611 0202; daily 12.30–3.30pm, 6.30–11.30pm; ££££; metro: Dhaula Kuan; map p.136 A2

The best, and most expensive, modern European food that the city has to offer, and certainly the only place where your meal will be served in a stationary railway carriage. The set menus are a very good (and cheaper) place to start, while the first-class ingredients are worked into delicious classic dishes. A place to dress up for, and to reserve in advance.

Wasabi

Taj Mahal, 1 Mansingh Road; tel: 2302 6162; daily 12.30–2.45pm, 7–11.30pm; £££; metro: Dhaula Kuan; map p.137 D2

This newly opened Japanese sushi and sake bar (a spin-off from the Taj in Mumbai) has caused a bit of a stir with some of the best raw fish in

Price per person for an average meal:
£ under Rs 200
££ Rs 200–500
£££ Rs 500–1,000
££££ Over Rs 1,000

the capital. The sake cocktails can be a bit hit and miss, and the whole experience is one guaranteed to drain your purse or wallet, but for sushi addicts it is well worth checking out.

Lodi Gardens and Nizamuddin

The Big Chill

35 and 68A Khan Market; tel: 4175 7588; daily noon–11.30pm; £–££; metro: Khan Market; map p.137 D2

Long standing and popular, The Big Chill is a small chain of cafés where the emphasis is a bit more on the food than just sitting with a coffee. Laid-back and friendly, there is a good selection of international dishes (burgers, pasta and Mexican dishes) as well as some yummy cakes and great ice cream. Also at F38, East of Kailash.

Dilli Haat

Opposite INA Market, Aurobindo Marg; tel: 2467 8812; daily 11am–10pm; £; metro: INA; map p.138 C4

The 'Foods of India' complex here has very cheap and clean stalls, run by different state tourist development corporations. An easy way to conduct a culinary tour of India and a good place to try unusual dishes, such as Minicoy fish curry or food from the Northeast.

Flavors

51–4C Moolchand Flyover Complex, Defence Colony; tel: 2464 5644; daily noon–11.30pm; £££; metro: Lajpat Nagar; map p.139 D4

Italian-owned and run, Flavors dishes up some of the most authentic Italian cuisine in town. The portions are huge but hard to resist, and the desserts lovely. The garden terrace is still the place to sit, making this a great place for lunch, and the space means it is also a good place to bring children.

The Kitchen

Middle Lane, 75 Khan Market; tel: 4175 7960; daily 11am–

Left: chic design at the Lodi Garden Restaurant.

metro: Jor Bagh; map p.137 D1
One of the city's only seafood specialists, and easily the best. Fish is flown in daily, so you need not fret about freshness. Although there is a lot on the menu, the best preparations are those from South India and Southeast Asia.

Sagar
18 Defence Colony Market; tel: 2433 3658; daily 8am–11pm; £; metro: Lajpat Nagar; map p.139 D4
This is just one of the best-known of a city-wide chain of very popular, and extremely clean, South Indian restaurants (some of the other central outlets can be found at Janpath, Lodi Road, Akhbar Road and Connaught Place). Good *thalis*, *dosas* and coffee.
Swagat,(tel: 2433 0930) a nearby Konkan seafood restaurant under the same management, is also good.

Threesixty
Oberoi, Dr Zakir Hussain Marg; tel: 2436 3030; daily 7am–1am; ££££; metro: JLN Stadium; map p.137 D2
One of the city's hippest restaurants, with a justly popular contemporary interior. The glass-fronted kitchens produce an amazing variety of Japanese, Continental – including good pizzas – and Indian delicacies before your eyes. Although it's not cheap, Threesixty is quite an experience, and the buffet lunch and Sunday brunch are a bargain.

South Delhi
Kasbah
N2 Market, Greater Kailash I; tel: 4163 5000; daily 12.30–3pm, 7.30–11.30pm; ££££; metro: East

11pm; ££; metro: Khan Market; map p.137 D2
This space cannot seat more than about 30 people, but it still manages to feel intimate without being cramped. The large menu on the wall displays a range of inventive – and tasty – Mediterranean, Indian and East Asian dishes such as sushi, linguini and noodles, as well as a couple of unexpected pleasures like Irish stew and grilled sausages.

Lodi – The Garden Restaurant
By Gate 1, Lodi Gardens, Lodi Road; tel: 2465 5054; daily 11am–3pm, 7–10.45pm; £££–££££; metro: Jor Bagh; map p.137 C1
This restaurant has a beautiful location in Lodi Gardens. The terrace overlooking the gardens and the outside seating under the trees are the biggest draw, although the Mediterranean food comes a close second. Sunday brunch makes for a particularly pleasant experience, though reservations are essential.

Left: laid-back and friendly at The Big Chill.

Mamagoto
1st Floor, 53 Middle Lane, Khan Market; tel: 4516 6060; daily 12.30pm–11.30pm (main courses only after 7pm); £££; metro: Khan Market; map p.137 D2
The minimalist interior belies the adventurous menu at this Southeast Asian eatery, where the emphasis is on fun and discovery. It's certainly one of the most varied menus of its kind in Delhi, and the quality of the food and excellent service have made it deservedly popular since its 2010 opening.

Ploof
13 Main Market, Lodi Colony; tel: 2463 4666; daily 11am–3.30pm, 7pm–1am; £££–££££;

Some of the very finest food to be had in Delhi can be found in the restaurants of its five-star hotels. If you are after Indian dishes then the Dum Phukt and Bukhara at the Maurya are superb, while the Chinese restaurants at the Taj Palace and the Hyatt Regency are world-class. Many of the five-stars also put on a good buffet brunch and lunch, perfect for a lazy Sunday.

of Kailash; map p.139 D3

Kasbah is a collection of restaurants, a café and a bar, all in the same building. Chic, modern interiors draw in the local in-crowd, as does the decent food. **Zaffran** concentrates on India, notably meat-heavy Avadhi, dishes to good effect, while **Spago** and the **Café de Paris** concentrate on Italian and 'French' dishes respectively. The last two are both fine, in a sort of 'nice ambience, food is OK' sort-of-way, while Zaffran scores a bit higher in the food stakes.

SEE ALSO CAFÉS AND BARS, P.31

Oh! Calcutta

E Block, International Trade Towers, Nehru Place; tel: 2646 4180; daily noon–3.15pm, 7–11.15pm; £££; metro: Nehru Place; map p.139 E3

Delhi's first real attempt at bringing the cuisine of West Bengal to the capital's diners has been a great success. This is first and

foremost a seafood restaurant, and particularly recommended are the *kakra chingri bhapa*, steamed crab-and-prawn cakes flavoured with lime and mustard, along with that Bengali staple *hilsa* and the wonderful *dal* and vegetable dishes.

Park Baluchi

Inside the Deer Park, Hauz Khas Village, New Delhi; tel: 2696 9829; daily noon–midnight; £££; metro: Hauz Khas; map p.138 B3

A relaxed and attractive restaurant serving rich – meat-heavy – Mughlai and Afghan dishes. The glass-backed building is in a lovely setting on the edge of the park.

Right: nice interiors reign at Kasbah.

Punjabi by Nature

11 PVR Priya Complex, Basant Lok, Vasant Vihar; tel: 4151 6666; daily 12.30–11.30pm; £££; metro: Hauz Khas; map p.138 A3

Perhaps the best Punjabi cuisine in Delhi. The food at this lively place gets consistently rave reviews, and is hugely popular with local diners. Great fun, rib-sticking and well worth booking ahead. There are also branches in Noida and Gurgaon.

SETZ

DLF Emporio Mall, 4 Nelson Mandela Marg, Vasant Kunj; tel: 4311 9999; daily noon–1am; £££; metro: Hauz Khas, map p.138 A1

Boasting no fewer than seven open kitchens, this is an exceptional choice for multi-cuisine dining, with North Indian, Thai, Coastal Indian, Chinese, Arabic, European and Japanese cuisines to choose from. It's a relaxing space and the quality of food impressive given the range on offer.

Mehrauli and Tughlaqabad

Dakshin

The Sheraton, District Centre, Saket; tel: 4266 1122; daily 12.30–12.45pm, 7.30–11.45pm; ££££; metro: Saket; map p.138 C1

This upmarket South Indian is not the place to try *dosas* and *uttapams* – you are better off going to Sagar or Saravana Bhavan for those – but excellent for more unusual meat dishes from Chettinad or fish from coastal Kerala and Karnataka. Do give the fiery offerings from Andhra a try as well.

Left: Threesixty at the Oberoi, *see p.117.*

Diva

M8, M Block Market, Greater Kailash II; tel: 2921 5673; daily 12.30–3pm, 7.30–11pm; ££££; metro: Kalkaji Mandir; map p.139 E2

This chic little Italian restaurant serves up some excellent – and authentic – food. There is a refreshing concentration on simple dishes, many of them vegetarian, which let the flavours come through. It also has one of the city's best selection of Italian wines.

IndoChine

Qutb Golf Course, Aurobindo Marg, Lado Sarai; tel: 2952 3330; daily noon–4pm, 8pm–1am; ££££; metro: Saket; map p.138 C1

Delhi's latest Southeast Asian restaurant has taken over the mantle from Thai Wok in the Qutb area. Nicely located, it is a good place to find Vietnamese, particularly noodle soups, and Singaporean dishes that you may not encounter elsewhere in Delhi.

Magique

F5–6, Eastern Court, Sadulajab, Garden of the Five Senses, Mehrauli–Badarpur Road; tel: 3271 6767; daily 12.30–3.30pm, 7.30–11.30pm; £££–££££; metro: Qutab Minar

A recent arrival on the Delhi scene and instantly popular, perhaps due to its great location in the Garden of the Five Senses. The inventive East and Southeast Asian food is a winner, and the open-air seating delightful. Phone for a reservation before making the long trek south.

Olive Bar & Restaurant

One Style Mile, Kalka Das Marg, Mehrauli; tel: 2957 4444; daily 12.30–3.30pm, 7.30–11.30pm; metro: Qutab Minar, map p.138 B1.

Recently re-opened in its original location, this is one of Delhi's best Mediterranean eateries, offering great ambience, attentive service and some exquisitely prepared food. Reservations essential.

> Although India held out for longer than most places, it has now embraced Western fast food with a rapacious appetite. Branches of McDonald's, Pizza Hut and Domino's can be found in every major city, and Delhi is no exception. Visit them if you must, but bear in mind that their offerings have been changed to cater to Indian tastes, and that local street vendors *(see the street food box on p.52)* and indigenous chains such as Nirula's dish up better food.

Smoke House Grill

2 VIPPS Centre, LSC Masjid Moth, Greater Kailash II; tel: 4143 5530; daily 12.30–3pm, 7.30pm–1am; ££££; Nehru Place; map p.139 E2

Fusion food is taking Delhi by storm, and not only in a 'Chinjabi' way; this restaurant – sister to a famous outlet in Mumbai – is currently top of the list. Rather self-conciously chic, it is where Delhi's 'it' crowd can be seen tucking into well-prepared Mediterranean/Asian/Mexican dishes (some more hit-and-miss than others; use your own judgement – if it sounds odd it will probably taste odd). Worth it for the good selection of drinks and the atmosphere alone.

Gurgaon

Konomi

The Trident, 443 Phase V, Udyog Vihar, Gurgaon; tel: 95124-245 0505; daily 12.30–3.30pm, 7.30–11pm; ££££; metro: IFFCO Chowk

Right up there with some of the priciest restaurants in Delhi, the Konomi does, however, serve some of the best sushi and sashimi in the city. If you are staying out in Gurgaon or near the airport then it is definitely worth a visit.

119

Shopping

Delhi is a shopper's paradise, from books and food, to clothes, to interior design, to art and jewellery – they can all be found in the city. Some of these are dealt with elsewhere in the book, for clothes and jewellery under Fashion, for books under Literature and Theatre, and for food under Food and Drink. Below are the main shopping areas, advice on what to look for, opening times, bargaining (at times, an essential Delhi tool) and the best places to shop for interesting souvenirs. India is famous for its craft work, and craft items (some of them of very high quality) make some of the most interesting buys.

Opening Hours

While some establishments shut later than others, nowhere opens early. Even government office hours vary, but 10am–6pm is a good rule of thumb. However, it's probably not worth arriving anywhere or starting your shopping trip until 11am – although things are slowly changing, Indian shops and offices still tend to crank into life slowly, with a cup of tea and a look through the newspaper essential precursors to the working day. Lunch hours are rigidly observed, and the arrival of a cup of *chai* will signal a pause in proceedings no matter how urgent the case in hand. If you want to look at the shops in them, museums and galleries are generally closed on Monday.

Where to Shop
Connaught Place

Connaught Place was built as the commercial centre of Lutyens's new city. Nowa-

Shops normally close for one day a week – known as the 'weekly off' – according to the market in which they are located. The general rule is that those markets that lie inside the Inner Ring Road close on a Monday, those outside on a Tuesday, although there are exceptions. The more central markets – Connaught Place for example – close on a Sunday.

days it is full of restaurants, Western sports shops and places trying to lure tourists. It is probably best to avoid

shopping here as the prices tend to be inflated. Also avoid the tourist traps in the underground Palika Bazaar. Connaught Place does, however, have a number of useful 24-hour ATMs.

Close to Connaught Place are the government-run crafts emporia which have good-quality items at fixed prices.

Old Delhi Bazaars

Between Chandni Chowk and Chawri Bazaar are the bazaars of Old Delhi. Running south off Chandni Chowk, just past the Jain

Right: a colourful array of crafts and household items in the government emporia.

Left: Select Citywalk Mall in South Delhi.

Block Markets are particularly good for clothing and home accessories), and **Lajput Nagar Central Market** for crafts and Indian clothing. For more traditional items and contemporary art the **Hauz Khas Village Complex** is a good bet, having recently gone through a resurgence in popularity.

South Delhi is home to a number of swish, air-conditioned malls. These are the hunting grounds for the young and affluent, who come to shop in branches of Western chain stores such as Debenhams, Marks & Spencer, Adidas and Nike. For most visitors there will be little point in visiting these to shop in places that are the same as back home. The upmarket **Select Citywalk Mall** (www.selectcitywalk.com) in Saket and **Emporio Mall** (www.dlfemporio.com) in Vasant Kunj are amongst the best that South Delhi has to offer. However, if it is truly huge malls you are craving, then head for Gurgaon. Here you will find, among others, **Gurgaon Ambi Mall** and the enormous new **Mall of**

Mandir, is **Dariba Kalan**, the jeweller's street, once famous for its gold but now mostly selling silver. **Katra Neel**, west of the Town Hall on Chandni Chowk, is a warren of small shops selling fabrics, particularly silk, by the metre. **Nai Sarak**, which runs between Chandni Chowk and Chawri Bazaar, has bookshops, mostly of educational publications. By the Jama Masjid is the extraordinary spare car-parts bazaar, not much use to the general visitor but still worth a look for the sheer spectacle.

The Colony Markets and Shopping Malls

On the edge of Chanakyapuri is a chic shopping complex called **Santushti**, run by the Airforce Wives' Association. Here there are a number of fabric and design shops all catering to Delhi's elite, with prices to match. To the east are the prime shopping areas of **Khan Market** and **Lodi Colony**, with everything from books to high-end fashion. Other 'colony' markets worth visiting are **South Extension** (western brands), **Greater Kailash Part I** (N and M

121

Above: cars line up outside the shops of Khan Market.

India (see www.gurgaon shoppingmalls.com for a full list).

Connaught Place

Baba Kharak Singh Marg Emporia
Mon–Sat 10am–7pm; metro: Rajiv Chowk; map p.136 C4

Baba Kharak Singh Marg, near Connaught Place, is where all state-government-run crafts emporia can be found. Each state has a handicrafts commission which runs a series of shops, and most of these are represented in Delhi. The pavements have recently been tidied up and widened, making negotiating your way between the shops more pleasant. Among the best of the emporia are: **Cauvery** (Karnataka) with good silks; **Poompuhar** (Tamil Nadu) with some exquisite, but expensive, bronzes; the **Handicrafts Development Corporation**, with lots of silks; **Lepakshi** (Andhra Pradesh) with good gold and pearl jewellery; **Rajasthali** (Rajasthan), with a very large and well-presented selection of everything from fabrics to

jewellery; and **Gurjari** (Gujarat) with an excellent selection of cotton textiles.

Central Cottage Industries Emporium
Jawahar Vyapar Bhawan, Janpath; tel: 2332 3825; www.cottageemporium.in; Daily Mon–Sat 10am–7pm; metro: Rajiv Chowk; map p.137 C4

This is the government-run central emporium that sells a huge variety of crafts from all over the country. The fixed prices and wide variety of goods, spread over six floors, make it a good place to start looking, or to visit if you are in a hurry and need a one-stop shop. It is a particularly good place to buy fabrics.

Kamala
Gallery 1, Rajiv Gandhi Handi-crafts Bhavan, Baba Kharak Singh Marg; tel: 6596 9600; www.craftscouncilofindia.org; Mon–Sat 10am–6.30pm; metro: Rajiv Chowk; map p.136 C4

This is the outlet for the Crafts Council of India, and the items on sale are of a suitably high standard. This is the place to look if you want something slightly out of the ordinary.

Khadi Bhavan
24 Regal Building, Connaught Place; tel: 2336 0902; Gramshilpa, 1 Baba Kharak Singh Marg; tel: 2336 0902; www.kvic.org.in; Mon–Sat 10.30am–6.30pm; metro: Rajiv Chowk; map p.137 C4

These are the two Delhi outlets of the *khadi* movement – handmade fabrics, cosmetics and items for the home, inspired by the ideas of Gandhi. Some of the hand-spun and hand-woven fabrics are exquisite.

Rajpath and Chanakyapuri

Crafts Museum
Pragati Maidan, Bhairon Road; tel: 2337 1641; www.national

Outside of government emporia and the more exclusive shops, it is customary to bargain. The classic strategy is to offer half what is being asked by the vendor and slowly move up to about two-thirds of the original price. Don't start bargaining unless you really want the item.

craftsmuseum.nic.in; Tue–Sun July–Sept 9.30am–5pm, Oct–June 9.30am–6pm; entrance charge; metro: Pragati Maidan; map p.137 E2

The crafts museum has an excellent shop that is worth a visit if you are looking for presents, toys or handicrafts.

Good Earth
18 Santushti Shopping Arcade; tel: 2410 0108; www.goodearth india.com; Mon–Sat 10am–6.30pm; metro: Race Course; map p.136 B2

Probably the most popular design chain in India, this chic shop sells all manner of tempting goodies for the house, from cushions to marble fountains, with a much more contemporary feel than items in the crafts emporia. Also at Khan Market (daily 11am–7.30pm), and a huge flagship store at Select Citywalk Mall, Saket (daily 11am–9pm).

SEE ALSO PAMPERING, P.97

Lodi Gardens and Nizamuddin

Anokhi
32 Khan Market; tel: 2460 3423; www.anokhi.com; Mon–Sat 10am–8pm; metro: Khan Market; map p.137 D2

Long a favourite with visitors and Delhiites alike, Anokhi was founded by Faith and John Singh to try to preserve some of the crafts of Rajasthan. Although well known for their easy cotton clothing they also produce home-furnishing fabrics, many block-printed using traditional techniques. Also in the Santushti Complex and N Block Market, Greater Kailash 1.

Dilli Haat

Opposite INA Market, Aurobindo Marg; tel: 2611 9055; www.delhitourism.nic.in; daily 10am–8pm; entrance charge; metro: INA; map p.138 C4

Set up by Delhi Tourism, this craft 'fair' (or *haat*) has over 60 stalls selling handicrafts from all over the country. The stallholders rotate, so it is worth paying a visit even if you have been before. The range of goods on offer is large, from papier mâché boxes to *dhurris* (rugs) and *saris*. There is also the popular food village here.

SEE ALSO RESTAURANTS, P.116

Fabindia

Central Hall, above Shops 20–21, Khan Market; tel: 4368 3100; www.fabindia.com; daily 10am–8pm; metro: Khan Market; map p.137 D2

Like Anokhi, Fabindia uses Indian craftworkers to produce its fabrics and home furnishings. Now a hugely successful chain, it not only sells clothes (for which it is very popular) but also attractive furniture, tableware, fabrics and toiletries. There are also branches at, among other places: B28 Connaught Place; 5, 7 and 14 N Block Market, Greater Kailash I; Karol Bagh; Lajpat Nagar and Vasant Kunj.

INTACH Heritage Shop

71 Lodi Estate; tel: 2469 2774; www.intach.org; Mon–Sat 10am–6pm; metro: Khan Market; map p.137 D2

The shop of the Indian Trust for Art and Cultural Heritage has a great range of crafts, sourced from workers all over the country. Well worth a visit for more unusual gifts.

Moon River

D16 Defence Colony; tel: 4161 7103; www.moonriverstore.com; daily 10.30am–7pm; metro: Lajpat Nagar; map p.139 D4

Perhaps Delhi's best design shop, selling top-end Indian design and very chic imported goods from Europe. If it is good-looking and expensive, you will find it here (and that goes not only for the clientele).

Oma

8A Khan Market; tel: 4359 7192; www.omaliving.com; daily 11am–7.30pm; metro: Khan Market; map p.137 D2

Oma is where you come to find top-end Indian design, some of it exquisite, some of it quirky. They also stock items from Scandinavian designers which, as you can imagine, are not cheap in Delhi.

South Delhi

Survey of India Map Sales Office

Next to IIT Gate, Shaheed Jeet Singh Marg; tel: 2696 2819; www.surveyofindia.gov.in; Mon–Fri 9am–5pm; metro: Rajiv Chowk; map p.137 C4

This is where you can pick up large-scale government maps of the country (NB: any maps over 1:250,000 may not be exported, but they may be used while you are in India).

The Carpet Cellar

1 Anand Lok, Khel Gaon Marg, Siri Fort Road; tel: 4164 1777; www.carpetcellar.com; Mon–Sat 10am–6pm; metro: Green Park; map p.139 C2

India produces some superb carpets, mostly in Kashmir, but this long-established shop also has carpets and kilims from Iran, Turkey and Central Asia.

Left: home furnishings and toiletries at Fabindia.

Sport

All of India is cricket mad, and Delhi is no exception. However, that is not the sum total of the city's sporting life. Delhi hosted the 2010 Commonwealth Games, and the city authorities used this excuse to tidy up the city and to push through a number of urgently needed infrastructure projects. As well as spectator sports, Delhi has some opportunities for those needing exercise to stretch their muscles. Its parks are good places to go running, while there are swimming pools at most of the five-star hotels, a posh golf course as well as tennis courts on offer.

The **Indian Premier League** (inevitably, contracted to IPL; www.iplt20.com) launched in 2008 to great excitement from India's millions of cricket fans. The franchises for the 20/20 teams were auctioned off for exorbitant fees and were snapped by India's rich and famous, including a number of Bollywood film stars (including Shah Rukh Khan and Preity Zinta). The floodlit matches are played with a razzmatazz that seems more akin to that which accompanies games of American football than cricket. However, it has gone down a storm. The local team are the Delhi Daredevils (www.delhidaredevils.com), whose franchise cost a cool US$84 million. They play out of Firoz Shah Kotla Stadium *(see right)* and have fared reasonably well so far, making the semi-final stage twice. The star of the team is Indian batsman Virender Sehwag.

Chess

India enjoys an excellent worldwide reputation for chess, with the current world champion, Viswanathan Anand, a Chennai native. Delhites are fond of the game; impromptu matches can be seen in parks and cafés all over the city, but if you're after something more formal visit www.delhichess.com.

Cricket

Much like the rest of India, Delhi is cricket-mad – even more so after the national team triumphed in the locally-hosted Cricket World Cup in 2011. International matches and those of the Indian Premier League *(see box, left)* are currently played at the Firoz Shah Kotla Stadium, which has been going since 1883. It has recently undergone a facelift and redevelopment, with the capacity increasing from 35,000 to over 60,000 and floodlighting put in place for the Cricket World Cup. You will not be able to avoid the game, as less formal matches take place in Delhi's parks every minute of the day, every day of the year.

Firoz Shah Kotla Stadium Bahadur Shah Zafar Marg; tel: 2331 9323; metro: Pragati Maidan; map p.135 D1

One of the smaller venues for cricket in the country, but with a lot of history. Perhaps its most famous hour in recent years was when Anil Kumble took 10 wickets in an innings against Pakistan in 1999, a world record. It is now home to the Delhi Daredevils of the Indian Premier League.

Golf

Delhi's posh golf club is slap bang in the middle of the city, and is replete with a Mughal-era tomb and numerous species of trees and birds. There is an 18- and 9-hole course, both of which can be booked by non-members of the club (the club is one of the great social gathering grounds for the city's 'great and good'). There is an amusing account of the club's history on its website. To book a slot in advance, which is essential, contact:

Delhi Golf Club Dr Zakir Hussain Marg, New Delhi; tel: 2430 7100; www.delhigolfclub.org; metro: Khan Market; map p.137 D2

Commonwealth Games 2010

The bagging of the 2010 Commonwealth Games was a big coup for Delhi and has considerably raised the profile of other sports than cricket in the capital, especially following one of the country's best hauls of medals ever at the Beijing Olympics, including India's first ever gold, and then an unprecedented 101 medals at the Delhi games themselves. The city's stadia were all given a make-over to bring them up to scratch for the games, and a new **Athletes Village** was built on the Trans-Yumana/Noida border. The centrepiece of the games was be the completely rebuilt **Jawarharlal Nehru Stadium** near Lodi Colony. For more information see www.cwgdelhi 2010.org.

The Men's Hockey World Cup 2010

As if bagging the Commonwealth Games were not enough, 2010 also saw the city play host to the Men's Hockey World Cup. Matches took place in the Dayan Chand National Stadium at the eastern end of Rajpath.

The **Delhi Half Marathon** is held each year, usually some time in November to avoid the summer heat. If you fancy having a go, check the details on http://adhm.procamrunning.in. Also on offer are a 4-km seniors' race and a 7-km run.

Running

There are plenty of opportunities for running in Delhi's parks, and you will find yourself in company in the early mornings and evenings. Lodi Gardens is particularly popular, as is Nehru Park in Chanakyapuri. Check out www.runningandliving.com.

Swimming

If you fancy a swim (and your hotel does not have a pool), your best bet is to head for one of the city's posh hotels, some of which will – for a hefty fee – allow non-residents to use their pool for the day. Of the other pools in the city, the best are probably the the ones at Siri Fort and

Pacific Sports Complex, close to Greater Kailash I 'N' Block Market.

SEE ALSO FORTS, P.56; SHOPPING, P.121

Tennis

If you fancy a game, head for the Delhi Lawn Tennis Association in Safdarjang Enclave. There are numerous courts, and it is possible to hire one if you contact them in advance: **Delhi Lawn Tennis Assoc. R.K. Khanna Tennis Stadium, 1 Africa Avenue; tel: 2617 6280; www.aitatennis.com; map p.138 B3**

They also have professional coaching, a pool and gym.

Right: Western sportswear is now widely available in Delhi.

Transept

गन्तव्य स्थान \ Destination
Kashmere Gate-M
कश्मीरी गेट

Transport

Getting to and around Delhi has never been easier: there are many daily flights now operating between India and the UK and US. The city has always had good options for public transport – including the ubiquitous auto rickshaws – but now it is even easier to find your way around with the completion of the impressive new metro network. One of India's most successful infrastructure projects, it has revolutionised the transport system in Delhi, and its cheap, quick and clean trains should be your first choice for negotiating the sometimes chaotic and crowded city.

Getting To

BY AIR

The vast majority of visitors arrive in India by air, with Delhi and Mumbai Airports the major entry points. The national carrier is Air India (www.airindia.com), but other carriers that have daily flights between the UK (where many transatlantic passengers can change) and India include British Airways (www.ba.com), Virgin Atlantic (www.virginatlantic.com), Jet Airways (www.jetairways.com) and Kingfisher (www.flykingfisher.com). Discounts are often available during the off-peak season, so it is worth making enquiries. Many long-haul flights arrive in Delhi between midnight and 6am. NB: It is advisable to check in for flights to and from India as early as possible, as flights are often overbooked.

TO/FROM THE AIRPORT

Indira Gandhi International Airport (IGIA Terminal Three; tel: 0124 337 6000; www.newdelhiairport.in) is 19km (12 miles)

Above: an auto waits in Hauz Khas Village.

southwest of the city centre; the domestic terminal (Terminal One; tel: 0124 337 6000) is 5km (3 miles) closer to town at Palam. The impressive new international terminal, which has already won a number of awards, was opened in 2010 in an attempt to keep up with the huge growth in both domestic and international air traffic, and the situation becomes particularly severe during January, when fog prevents planes from taking off until 11am, by which time there's a huge backlog.

The best transport option

While autos can be the most convenient way to get around the centre of town, it is often hard for visitors to negotiate a fair price for their journey. The Delhi government is wise to the problem and has put an extremely useful fare calculator online (www.delhigovt.nic.in/revised_auto_rickshaw_fares.asp), which will give a good indication of what to pay the driver.

into the city is now the metro, with the airport line having opened in February 2011. Alternatively there is the very reasonable, but slow, bus and a number of pre-paid taxi services; there are numerous kiosks to the left as you come out of security, but ignore them all: the official taxi service, and the cheapest, has its office just outside the door to the right as you come out.

It is also worth remembering that luggage should not be left to travel round and round the carousel, but taken off and arranged on the floor next to the relevant belt.

Left: getting around is easy on the new metro system.

advise you on how likely you are to get a reservation. Tatkal trains (marked with a 'T' in timetables) have a certain number of reservations held back, which become available one day in advance for an extra charge, but you forfeit the full amount in case of cancellation.

INDIAN RAILWAYS WEBSITES

For general information:
www.indianrailways.gov.in
For timetables, fares and the current status of trains and your ticket:
www.indianrail.gov.in
To buy tickets online:
www.irctc.co.in
www.cleartrip.com

Getting Around

BUSES

While there are a huge number of buses plying the roads of Delhi, the effort required to discover their destination (generally signposted in Hindi), and the fact that they're packed to the gills during rush hour, mean that visitors tend to be put off using them. In particular, the privately operated 'Blue Line' buses are notorious for causing accidents, and are responsible for not a few of

BY BUS

The majority of buses coming into Delhi from outlying areas arrive at the Inter State Bus Terminal near Kashmere Gate. However, this is by no means the most comfortable, or safe, way of travelling around the country and is best avoided unless you have no alternative.

BY TRAIN

Delhi's two main railway stations, New Delhi and Old Delhi, handle the vast majority of train traffic in and out of the city, although there are a number of smaller stations. Rail travel is safe, comfortable and by far the most atmospheric way to get around the country. Trains are slow compared to those in the West, and you are best sticking to the superfast Rajdhani or Shatabdi and Jan Shatabdi services if at all possible. Fares are generally low and, for the distances covered, a bargain. All carriages have both Western

and Indian-style toilets. If you are up to squatting on a moving train always use the Indian toilets as they are invariably cleaner and better-maintained.

It is essential that you book your ticket well in advance (the International Tourist Bureau at New Delhi railway station, tel: 2334 6804, is very helpful). If reservations are not available then certain trains have a tourist quota that may be available. Other options are to take a waitlisted ticket or the more assured reservation against cancellation (RAC); the booking clerk should be able to

Right: Delhi's crowded bus service.

Above: the old and the new.

the deaths that occur on the Delhi streets. The Delhi government-run buses (see www.dtc.nic.in for route information) are safer and more reliable, and the authorities have recently put in to service an entirely new fleet of modern buses to replace the old, rickety ones that used to ply the streets. On the plus side, fares are cheap, between Rs 2 and 10, and with the new bus fleet, some of which are air conditioned, this has become a more attractive way of getting around the city.

THE METRO
The much-expanded metro network (www.delhimetrorail.com; see also map opposite) is extremely useful. Easy to use, single fares operate by means of a 'token' which you hold by the reader at the start of your journey and feed into the machine at the automatic barrier when you exit the station. Fares are cheap, between Rs 6 and 22, and services run from 6am to 11pm. There are two 'tourist cards' that give unlimited travel for a specific

period. One is valid for 24 hours and costs Rs 70, the other is valid for three days and costs Rs 200. Both require a deposit of Rs 50 for the return of the card.

RICKSHAWS
Often the most convenient, and classically Indian, way of getting around town is by rickshaw. These come in two types: a cycle rickshaw (a tricycle with a seat for two people on the back), and a motorised three-wheeler known as an 'auto' (these, like the city buses, have all been converted to run on CNG, compressed natural gas).

Autos, like taxis, are supposed to use a meter. You should insist on this and get out if they refuse. Meter rates are subject to periodic changes, and extras for late-night journeys etc., which the driver should show you on a card. In popular tourist spots, during rush hour and bad weather, you may find it impossible to persuade the drivers to use the meter. A tactic that might work is to offer 'meter plus X' (the cost of the meter plus an extra amount). If not, you'll have to negotiate the fare (see box on p.126). After a short while in the city you will get a feel for what is acceptable, given that as a relatively well-off foreign tourist you are expected to pay a little more.

Some auto drivers might suggest that, for a fixed

amount, they take you around the sites for a whole day. This can be convenient and, if you bargain well, good value. Make sure that both of you understand what the price is and where you want to go (i.e. not via endless shops) before you set off.

Cycle rickshaws are more convenient in some places, like the very congested streets of Old Delhi. With these you should negotiate the fare before you set off.

TAXIS
Distinguishable by their black, yellow and green livery and yellow number plates, Delhi's taxis are generally difficult to flag down on the street. They gather at their transport company's kiosk, which can be found close to all the main markets or commercial areas. Rates are meant to be determined by meter, though a little persuasion is often required to ensure their use, drivers preferring to fix a rate before departure. A 50 percent surcharge is added at night.

With constant hikes in fuel prices, charges may often be higher than indicated on the meter. If so, this will be prominently stated in the taxi, and the driver will have a card showing the excess over the meter reading that can be legitimately charged.

Two companies that are reliable, honest and can be booked by phone are:
Allied Taxi Service
1 Jor Bagh, Lodi Colony, Lodi Road, near India Habitat Centre; tel: 2463 5501
Mega Cabs
Tel: 41414141;
www.megacabs.com
A true radio taxi service with AC cars and GPS navigation.

> India's roads are the most dangerous in the world, with over 130,000 deaths per year. So don't even think about hiring a car and driving yourself: leave it to the locals, who instinctively know the unwritten 'rules' of the road.

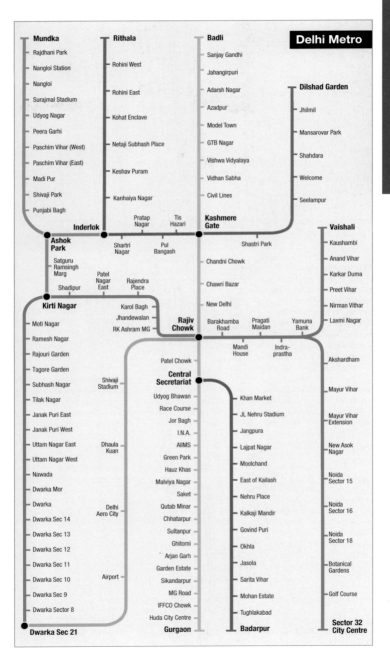

Delhi Metro

Mundka
- Rajdhani Park
- Nangloi Station
- Nangloi
- Surajmal Stadium
- Udyog Nagar
- Peera Garhi
- Paschim Vihar (West)
- Paschim Vihar (East)
- Madi Pur
- Shivaji Park
- Punjabi Bagh

Rithala
- Rohini West
- Rohini East
- Kohat Enclave
- Netaji Subhash Place
- Keshav Puram
- Kanhaiya Nagar

Badli
- Sanjay Gandhi
- Jahangirpuri
- Adarsh Nagar
- Azadpur
- Model Town
- GTB Nagar
- Vishwa Vidyalaya
- Vidhan Sabha
- Civil Lines

Dilshad Garden
- Jhilmil
- Mansarovar Park
- Shahdara
- Welcome
- Seelampur

Inderlok

Ashok Park

Pratap Nagar   Tis Hazari

Kashmere Gate

Vaishali
- Kaushambi
- Anand Vihar
- Karkar Duma
- Preet Vihar
- Nirman Vithar
- Laxmi Nagar

Satguru Ramsingh Marg

Shartri Nagar   Pul Bangash

Shastri Park

Shadipur

Patel Nagar East   Rajendra Place

Chandni Chowk

Chawri Bazar

Kirti Nagar
- Moti Nagar
- Ramesh Nagar
- Rajouri Garden
- Tagore Garden
- Subhash Nagar
- Tilak Nagar
- Janak Puri East
- Janak Puri West
- Uttam Nagar East
- Uttam Nagar West
- Nawada
- Dwarka Mor
- Dwarka
- Dwarka Sec 14
- Dwarka Sec 13
- Dwarka Sec 12
- Dwarka Sec 11
- Dwarka Sec 10
- Dwarka Sec 9
- Dwarka Sector 8

Karol Bagh
Jhandewalan
RK Ashram MG

Rajiv Chowk

New Delhi

Barakhamba Road   Pragati Maidan   Yamuna Bank

Mandi House   Indra-prastha

Akshardham

Patel Chowk

Central Secretariat

Shivaji Stadium

Udyog Bhawan
Race Course
Jor Bagh
I.N.A.
AIIMS
Green Park
Hauz Khas
Malviya Nagar
Saket
Qutab Minar
Chhatarpur
Sultanpur
Ghitorni
Arjan Garh
Garden Estate
Sikandarpur
MG Road
IFFCO Chowk
Huda City Centre

Gurgaon

Dhaula Kuan

Delhi Aero City

Airport

Khan Market
JL Nehru Stadium
Jangpura
Lajpat Nagar
Moolchand
East of Kailash
Nehru Place
Kalkaji Mandir
Govind Puri
Okhla
Jasola
Sarita Vihar
Mohan Estate
Tughlakabad

Badarpur

Mayur Vihar

Mayur Vihar Extension

New Asok Nagar

Noida Sector 15

Noida Sector 16

Noida Sector 18

Botanical Gardens

Golf Course

Sector 32 City Centre

Dwarka Sec 21

129

Walks

Although at first glance, with all its hectic traffic, Delhi does not seem the ideal place in which to go for a walk, many areas of the city offer fascinating places to wander through. As well as self-guided walks, there are special guided walks, often with a historical or cultural focus, to take advantage of. Birdwatchers should take themselves off to the city's parks or up onto the Ridge that runs from north to south across the western side of Delhi. Old Delhi, in particular, is a place that gives up its secrets only when explored on foot, as are some of the colonies of the south and their monuments.

It can get very hot in Delhi, especially in summer, so leave these walks for either the winter months or very early morning. Wear sturdy shoes, as Delhi's 'pavements' can be either non-existent or spring some nasty surprises on you such as sudden holes or bits of sharp iron that could cut open your feet. Also, carry a bottle of water and try and stick in the shade as much as possible. A good map is essential if you intend to set out on your own.
SEE ALSO ESSENTIALS, P.38

Old Delhi

If you want to explore this fascinating area in depth then get a copy of *Old Delhi: Ten Easy Walks (see box)*. However, one good walk is to explore the bazaars that surround **Chandni Chowk** (map p.135 D3). Start at the end nearest the Lal Qila (metro: Chandhi Chowk), turn left into Dariba Kalan, then right into **Kinari Bazaar**. This will bring you back onto Chandni Chowk itself. Carry on to the fabric bazaar of **Katra Neel** the other side of the Town Hall, and then

If you want to explore Old Delhi in more depth then go on foot then get hold of a copy of *Old Delhi: Ten Easy Walks*, by Gayner Barton and Lorraine Malone (Rupa & Co, 2006). This very useful guide to the confusing maze of streets in Old Delhi should be available in most good bookshops in the city.

take Nai Sarak opposite. At the end turn left into Chawri Bazaar, which will bring you out in front of the **Jama Masjid** (metro: Chawri Bazaar).
SEE ALSO RELIGIONS AND RELIGIOUS SITES, P.107; SHOPPING, P.121

Rajpath and Chanakyapuri

With its wide, open boulevards this district makes good sense to walk through. One of the very best walks, and most interesting, through Lutyens's Delhi is to start from **India Gate** (metro: Khan Market) and to walk straight down Rajpath (map p.137 D3/C3). On the way you will pass by the National Museum, and will also get a sense of North and South Blocks unfolding in front of

you as you get nearer to them. Finish by going up the slight rise of Raisina Hill to see through the gates of **Rashtrapati Bhavan** (metro: Central Secretariat).

A further walk could take you from the **Purana Qila** to **Humayun's Tomb** (map p.137 E3/E2). Start at the entrance to the Purana Qila (metro: Pragati Maidan), and walk left down Mathura Road for about 100 m/yds. Turn left into the colony of Sundar Nagar and carry on right to the edge of the colony and turn right. This will take you alongside the edge of Delhi Zoo. At the end of the long straight road, turn left into the small lane and then right at the first turning. This will bring you through the nurseries around the Sundarwala Burj and out onto Bharat Scouts and Guides Marg beside the entrance to Humayun's Tomb (metro: Pragati Maidan).
SEE ALSO FORTS, P.56; MONUMENTS, P.78

Lodi Gardens and Nizamuddin

One of the nicest walks in this area is through Lodi Gardens

Left: follow the signpost to designer fashion.

run some highly recommended walks though Delhi.

Delhi Heritage Walks
Tel: 9212534868; www.delhiheritagewalks.com
The most comprehensive service available, with 11 routes to choose from. There's a monthly walk schedule on the website.

India Habitat Centre
Habitat World, India Habitat Centre, Lodi Road; tel: 4366 3333; www.habitatworld.com
Check the programme here for all kinds of guided walks, from art galleries to archaeological sites to nature tours.

INTACH
The Indian National Trust for Art and Cultural Heritage, 71 Lodi Estate; tel: 2463 1818; www.intach.org
INTACH runs regular guided walks around Old Delhi, Nizamuddin, Hauz Khas, Lodi Gardens and Mehrauli Archaeological Park.

Below: walking through Lodi Gardens.

and down into Lodi Colony (map p.137 C2/D1). Start at the junction of South End Road and Amrita Shergil Marg at the northern end of the gardens (metro: Khan Market). Make your way south through the park, having a look at monuments en route, and exit just below **Muhammad Shah's Tomb** onto Lodi Road. Cross this – carefully – and carry straight on into **Lodi Colony** and its market full of designer shops (metro: Jor Baqh). An advantage of this route is that there are a couple of very good places to eat on the way.
SEE ALSO MONUMENTS, P.79; PARKS AND GARDENS, P.100

South Delhi

There are huge swathes of South Delhi to explore, but one of the most pleasant bits to mooch about in is **Hauz Khas Village** (map p.138 B3). Explore the backstreets and little boutiques here, then head for the **Tughlaq** *madrasa* and tomb and take a stroll around the tank which gives the area its name (metro: Green Park).
SEE ALSO MONUMENTS, P.80

Mehrauli

The other monument-rich area that almost demands to be explored on foot is Mehrauli Village (map p.138 A1). Coming from the Qutb Minar Complex (metro: Qutab Minar), on your right as you enter the village is the **Bhulbhulaiyan**. A little further on is a turning to the left, just before the *dargah* of **Bakhtiyar Kaki**; following this will bring you down to **Jamali Kamali**. Retrace your steps back to the main road through the village and hop into an auto (or, if you are feeling energetic, walk) down to the **Hauz-i-Shamsi** at the southern edge of Mehrauli, and take a walk around the tank.
SEE ALSO MONUMENTS, P.81

Guided Walks

While you can, of course, explore the city on foot on your own armed with a map and a guidebook, there are a number of places offering guided walks. These can be an excellent way of learning more about the city, as the guides will point out things you might miss on your own. The following organisations

Atlas

The following streetplan of Delhi makes it easy to find the attractions listed in the A–Z section. A selective index to streets and sights will help you find other locations throughout the city

Map Legend

Pedestrian area		(M)	Metro station
Notable building		🚏➕	Cathedral / church
Transport hub		⊕	Hospital
Park		🚌	Bus station
Hotel		ⓘ	Tourist information
Urban area		★	Sight of interest
Non urban area		⚊	Statue / monument
† † Cemetery			

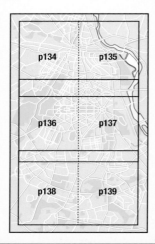

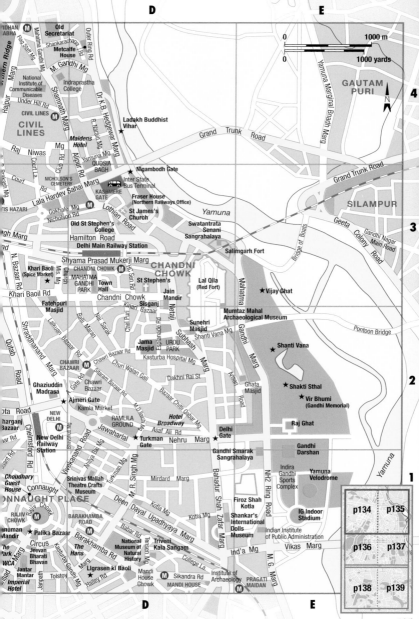

0   1000 m

0   1000 yards

GAUTAM
PURI

N

4

SILAMPUR

3

Southern Ridge

PIDHAN
ABHA

Old
Secretariat

Metcalfe
House

M. Gandhi Mg

Shankaracharya Rd

National
Institute of
Communicable
Diseases

Indraprastha
College

CIVIL LINES

CIVIL
LINES

Under Hill Rd

Maidens
Hotel

Raj
Niwas

Yamuna Mg

QUDSIA
BAGH

Ladakh Buddhist
Vihar

Grand   Trunk   Road

Grand Trunk Road

Yamuna Marginal Bridh Marg

Nigambodh Gate

Inter State
Bus Terminal

KASHMERE
GATE

Fraser House
(Northern Railways Office)

St James's
Church

Yamuna

Bridge of Boats

Geeta Colony Road

Gandhi Nagar
Main Road

NICHOLSON'S
CEMETERY

Lala Hardev Sahai Marg

Gokhale Mg

Nicholson Rd

Old St Stephen's
College

Hamilton Road

Swatantrata
Senani
Sangrahalaya

TIS HAZARI

Delhi Main Railway Station

Salimgarh Fort

Shyama Prasad Mukerji Marg

CHANDNI
CHOWK

Pontoon Bridge

Khari Baoli
(Spice Market)

CHANDNI CHOWK

St Stephen's

Lal Qila
(Red Fort)

★ Vijay Ghat

Mahatma Gandhi Marg

Khari Baoil Rd

MAHATMA
GANDHI
PARK

Town
Hall

Chandni Chowk

Jain
Mandir

Mumtaz Mahal
Archaeological Museum

Fatehpuri
Masjid

Sisganj
Bazaar

Kinari Bazaar

Sunehri
Masjid

Shanti Vana Mg

★ Shanti Vana

Shraddhanand Marg

Lalkuan Bazaar Rd

Chor Bazaar Rd

Ballimaran

Nai Sarak

Jama
Masjid

URDU
PARK

Subhash Marg

★ Shakti Sthal

Qutab Road

CHAWRI
BAZAAR

Gate Rd

Chawri Bazaar Rd

Churi Walan Gali

Kasturba Hospital Mg

Dakhni Rai St

Ghata
Masjid

Ghata Road

★ Vir Bhumi
(Gandhi Memorial)

Ghaziuddin
Madrasa

Chawri
Bazaar

Bazaar Chitli Qabar Mg

Arjan Road

Ajmeri Gate

Kamla Market

RAMLILA
GROUND

Hotel
Broadway

M J Road

Delhi
Gate

★ Raj Ghat

Gandhi
Darshan

Road

harganj
Bazaar

NEW
DELHI

Jawaharlal   Nehru   Marg

Asaf Ali Rd

★ Turkman
Gate

Gandhi Smarak
Sangrahalaya

aar Rd

New Delhi
Railway Station

Vivekanand Road

Bhavbhuti Marg

Mirdard   Marg

Bahadur Shah Zafar Marg

Indira
Gandhi
Sports
Complex

Yamuna
Velodrome

Chelmsford Rd

M.R. Singh Rd

Kotla Mg

Firoz Shah
Kotla

Yamuna

NH2 Ring Road

Choudhary
Guest
House

Connaught

CONNAUGHT PLACE

Srinivas Mallah
Theatre Crafts
Museum

Deen Dayal Upadhyaya Marg

Kotla Mg

Shankar's
International
Dolls Museum

IG Indoor
Stadium

RAJIV
CHOWK

BARAKHAMBA
ROAD

Babar Rd

Indian Institute
of Public Administration

Vikas   Marg

M. G. Road

anuman
Mandir

★ Palika Bazaar

Jeevan
Bharati
Bhavan

Barakhamba Rd

Triveni
Kala Sangam

Ind'a Mg

he
ark
WCA

Circus

The
Hans

National
Museum of
Natural History

Tansen Marg

College La.

Jantar
Mantar

Imperial
Hotel

Kasturba Gandhi Mg

Ligrasen ki Baoli

Hailey Rd

Mandi
House
Chowk

Sikandra Rd

Institute of
Archaeology

PRAGATI
MAIDAN

Tolstoy

Janpath

Mandi
House

p134	p135
p136	p137
p138	p139

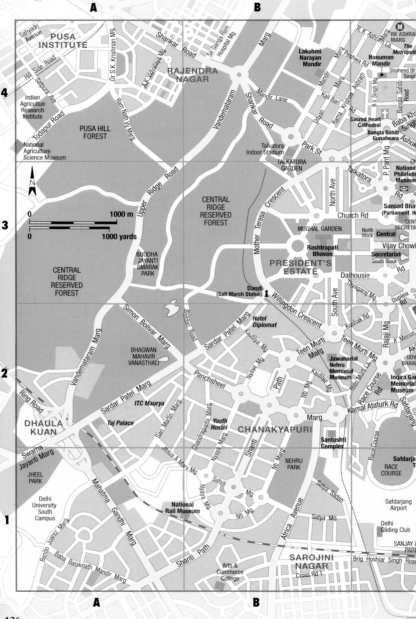

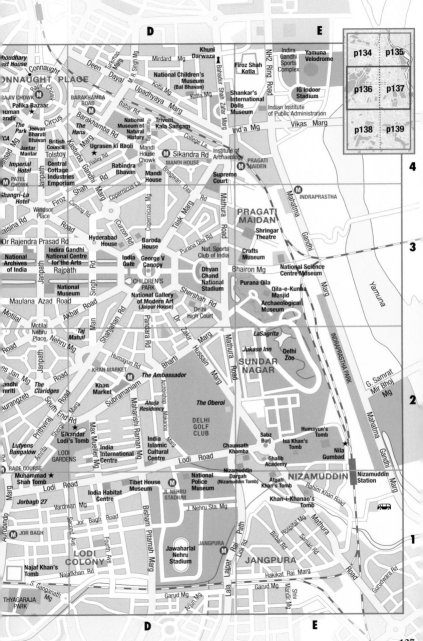

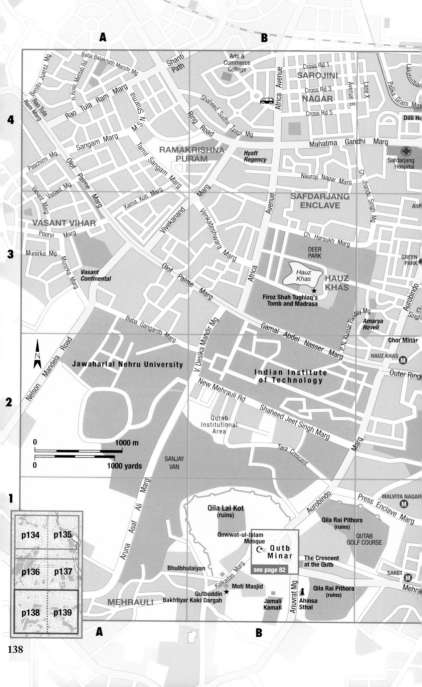

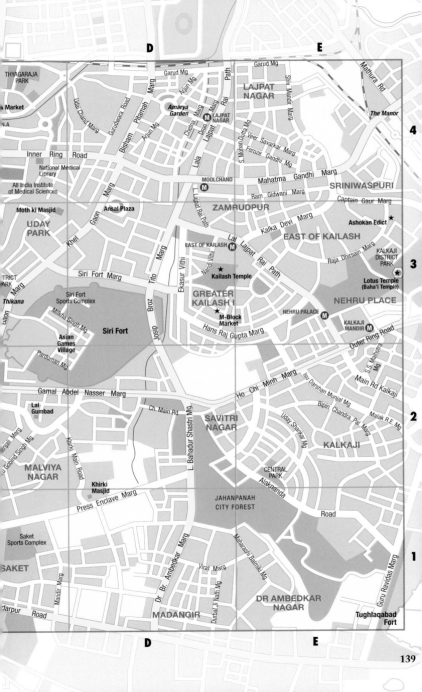

Index for Street Atlas

POINTS OF INTEREST

141

Index

Insight Smart Guide: Delhi
Written and compiled by: **Maria Lord**
Updated by: **Gavin Thomas**
Edited by: **Alyse Dar and Tom Le Bas**
Proofread and indexed by: **Neil Titman**
All pictures © APA/ Julian Love, Britta
Jaschinski and Henry Wilson except:
Istockphoto 92/93, 93B, 94, Alamy
17T, Fotolia 17B, 31B, Kobal 48T,
49B, 48/49.
Design Manager: **Steven Lawrence**
Art Editor: **Richard Cook**
Maps: **Phoenix Mapping, Mapping Ideas**
Series Editor: **Sarah Sweeney**

Second Edition 2011
First Edition 2009
©2011 Apa Publications (UK) Limited

Printed by CTPS-China
Worldwide distribution enquiries:
APA Publications GmbH & Co Verlag KG
(Singapore branch); 7030 Ang Mo Kio Ave 5,
08-65 Northstar @ AMK, Singapore
569880; email: apasin@singnet.com.sg
Distributed in the UK and Ireland by:
GeoCenter International Ltd; Meridian House,
Churchill Way West, Basingstoke, Hampshire,
RG21 6YR; email: sales@geocenter.co.uk
Distributed in the United States by:
Ingram Publisher Services
One Ingram Blvd, PO Box 3006, La Vergne,
TN 37086-1986; email: customer.
service@ingrampublisherservices.com
Distributed in Australia by:
Universal Publishers; PO Box 307,
St. Leonards, NSW 1590; email:

sales@universalpublishers.com.au
Contacting the Editors
We would appreciate it if readers would alert us
to errors or outdated information by writing to:
Apa Publications, PO Box 7910, London SE1
1WE, UK; fax: (44 20) 7403 0290;
email: insight@apaguide.co.uk
No part of this book may be reproduced,
stored in a retrieval system or transmitted in
any form or by any means (electronic,
mechanical, photocopying, recording or
otherwise), without prior written permission of
Apa Publications. Brief text quotations with
use of photographs are exempted for book
review purposes only. Information has been
obtained from sources believed to be reliable,
but its accuracy and completeness, and the
opinions based thereon, are not guaranteed.

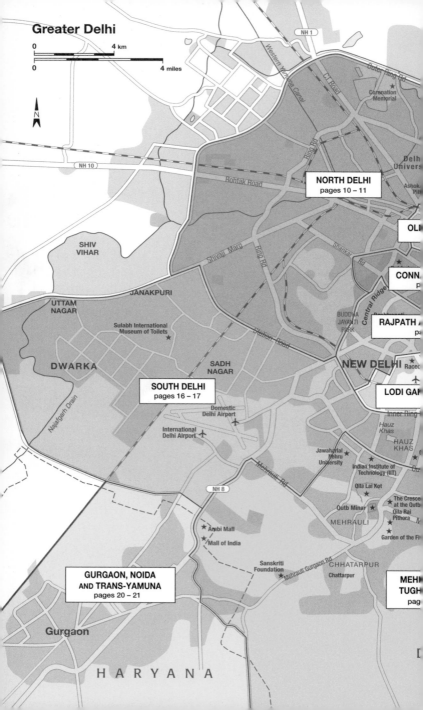

Greater Delhi

0   4 km

0   4 miles

N

NH 1

Western Yamuna Canal

GT Road

Outer Ring Rd

Coronation Memorial

Delhi University

Ashok Pill

NH 10

Ring Rd

Rohtak Road

NORTH DELHI
pages 10 – 11

OL

SHIV VIHAR

Shivaji Marg

Ring Rd

Shankar Rd

Central Ridge

BUDDHA JAYANTI PARK

CONN
p

JANAKPURI

UTTAM NAGAR

Sulabh International Museum of Toilets

Station Road

RAJPATH
pa

NEW DELHI ★ Racec

DWARKA

SADH NAGAR

SOUTH DELHI
pages 16 – 17

LODI GAR

Inner Ring

Najafgarh Drain

Domestic Delhi Airport

International Delhi Airport

Hauz Khas

**HAUZ
KHAS**

Mehrauli Rd

Jawaharlal Nehru University

Indian Institute of Technology (IIT)

Gtr

NH 8

Qila Lai Kot

The Crescent at the Qutb
Qila Rai Pithora

Qutb Minar ★

MEHRAULI

Garden of the Fi

Ambi Mall ★

Mall of India ★

Sanskriti Foundation

Mehrauli Gurgaon Rd

CHHATARPUR

Chattarpur

**MEH
TUGH**
pag

GURGAON, NOIDA
AND TRANS-YAMUNA
pages 20 – 21

Gurgaon

D

H A R Y A N A